What People Are Saying
From Modeling Clothes To Modeling Self...

"... As we all make our way through this journey called life, we are, on occasion blessed by crossing paths with those whose integrity and desire to do good is exceeded only by their unconditional love and genuine caring. Just such a person is Frannie ... I am certain that anyone fortunate enough to have the good pleasure of reading this divinely inspired book will, on every possible level – from the physical to the spiritual – be uplifted, empowered, enlivened and exhilarated."

Harvey Diamond
Author of *Fit for Life Not Fat for Life*
Co-Author of *Fit for Life & Fit for Life II*

"In each moment, we are modeling something. Sometimes it is fear. Sometimes it is love. The question is not, 'How can we get rid of our fear?' The question is 'How can we hold our fear with love?' The answer to that question can be found in these pages. And when you find it, you will feel its echo in your heart."

Paul Ferrini
Author of *Love Without Conditions*
and over 28 inspirational books on
love, forgiveness and healing.

"Frannie has been part of my life now for over twenty-five years. During that time I've had the great privilege of watching her grow into her experience of becoming an amazing instrument for God's love and truth. Her personal journey of healing, growth, miracles and transformation, told straight from her heart, will enlighten, teach, uplift and inspire you. The flow of energy in the very words themselves will go straight to your heart. Read this book – and if you allow it, Frannie's compelling story will open your heart to love and ultimately bring you closer to who you are as a divine being."

Janet Matthews
Co-author of *Chicken Soup for the Canadian Soul*

"Psychological insight may set the table, but nurturance and joy come from a loving heart and soul. Even some physicians nowadays are realizing the true art of Medicine as that of being healers of the body, mind and spirit. Then there are the exceptionally gifted healers like Frannie, who show us the power of spiritual energy as we bring our emotional selves back into oneness with our bodies. No mind-tripping here; not even meditation-tripping. Rather, she guides our making of peace with ourselves as a sacred experience of loving faith. With her, healing is a resurrection of our true self, unbroken, freed from illusions, strong and able to be all we can be."

Robert J. Mignone, M.D.
Teacher and clinician
Educated at Duke (M.D.)
Yale (Internal Medicine),
Cornell (Neurology), and
Harvard (Psychiatry)

"I couldn't put the book down. I got such a great feeling of being connected, and this wonderful presence of love and tranquility. It's like knowing you're in the right place again. Through her stories and experiences, Frannie empowers you in a way that makes you feel better about yourself and knowing what it's really all about. Great book!"

James H. Martin, DC, DACBN, FAAIM
Author of New Advances In Natural Health and Healing

"Frannie's deeply honest and courageous account of her personal journey will touch your heart. Her commitment to love and life light up every page. From Modeling Clothes to Modeling Self: A Journey of Remembering the Simple Truths of Love encourages each of us to connect to our own source of inner wisdom and Divine love."

Cindy Stone
Author of The Incidental Guru

For Jim:

Your heart
knows all that
is love.

Blessings to
you

Frannie ♡

Modeling Comps

FROM MODELING CLOTHES TO MODELING SELF:
A Journey of Remembering the Simple Truths of Love

FRANNIE HOFFMAN

ARAYASUN

Published by ARAYASUN Books
A Road Signs Productions Company

ARAYASUN

Published by ARAYASUN Books 2004
A Road Signs Productions Company
PO Box 374
Anna Maria, Florida 34216

Editing: Janet Matthews and Jodi Solomon
Cover Photography: Anna Bratt Photography
Cover Art: Frannie Hoffman
Cover Design: Jodi Solomon and Frannie Hoffman

ISBN: 0-9746938-0-4

Printed in Canada

DEDICATION

To my parents Susan and Phillip Hoffman – thank you for the gift of life, and the unconditional love you have always given me.

To my children, Luke and Lane Andrews, who are always reminding me of the simple truths of love. You mean everything to me.

To my beloved husband, Steven Kaluza – thank you for dancing, dreaming and diving into life with me. You believed in me even when I did not.

To my sisters: Colleen Smith, you are my mirror, a reflection of love, courage and strength – no one knows me as you do; Philomene Hoffman, thank you for reminding me to choose to live in this body and for inspiring me with your passionate voice that speaks deeply into my heart. To my brother Philip Hoffman, your vision and creative expression continually serve me and your gentle nature holds me even when we are not together.

To you all, my heart bows to your hearts.

CONTENTS

CONTENTS

Book 2: The Simple Truths of Love

ACKNOWLEDGMENTS

This book is a labor of love from my heart. It has been a full ten years in the making and along the way so many have helped to make the dream come true. I have been loved and supported and inspired by this world and beyond every step of the way. I am in such gratitude to the Divine Spirit that has embraced me throughout my whole life even when I did not feel it.

With my whole heart I thank Jodi Solomon who said yes to helping me complete this project and never forgot the vision. Your many talents and gifts have touched this book with the same love and affection with which I wrote it. I am overwhelmed and deeply touched by your commitment and encouragement. Without you this book would simply not have been finished.

Thank you Janet Matthews for your expertise in the final editing. You styled me 26 years ago in front of the camera and you are styling me now with the same love and dedication to the beauty of the finished product.

My dear friend and mentor Paul Ferrini. Your love and support continue to inspire me through your writings and our friendship.

Thank you Gary Zukav for your powerful words in Mt. Shasta that propelled me into fulfilling my life's purpose.

Thank you Harvey Diamond. Your wisdom on health and nutrition helped me to heal my physical body. I am blessed to call you my friend.

Jim Martin, your nurturing commitment to my health and brotherly love continue to touch me always; Fernando Ania, you opened me to another way to heal; Jim De Maio, with your loving kindness I was able to recognize my ego; Alain Menard thank you for always being there.

To Bob Andrews – no words can express my love and gratitude for the partnership we shared and the miraculous co-creation we birthed in our children. And to Bob's wife, Nancy, for your love, support and commitment to our children I am eternally grateful.

Thank you Viveka Von Rosen, Florence Semple and Merlelynn Dratch, who helped me with typing the original manuscript. Your input helped shape the course and direction of the final project.

To Chris Chalupa who moved from New York to help and inspire me to bring my gifts into the world. I am indebted for your help in the production of the guided meditation tapes.

I give thanks from the deepest part of my heart to all of my family and friends who have loved me and believed in me and continue to inspire me to be all that I can be. To Bruce Smith, my brother-in-law, you took me into your home and created a safe space for me to let go and re-write the chapters of my book; To Janine Marchessault, you blessed my life when you married my brother; to all of my nieces – Lindsay, Lauren, Jessica, Jessie, Alicia, Amber, Jennifer and Ashley – who continually bring me back to my youth and my aliveness. How sweet it is to be married into the Kaluza family – Dan & RoeAnn Kaluza, Sondra & Dan Hirssig, Mike & Julie Kaluza – your love and support touch my heart always.

To all my circles of women, men and children who have joined with me in meditation and prayer for all these years, as we have grown together in love and peace – we are always joined in heart wherever we journey to. Thank you for every hug and kiss. To my angel sisters, you know who you are. Your belief in me has always been deeply felt and has given me the courage to move myself and my gifts into the world.

Kristine and Jacques Gagne, you supported me in so many ways with your unending love and gifts from the heart. (I Love The Flower Girl)

To Boman Najme, who showed me a trusting, generous heart that loves without conditions. Thank you.

Jaye Brownewell, who transcribed and typed countless tapes; Joy Gardner, Mary Wirth, Ann Besterfield, Ticia Cousy, Haike Vaudry, Sondra Hirssig, Fay Huang, Brigette Hamm and Laurie Carah, who helped read the final manuscript. I needed your eyes and you gave with all your heart, as you always do through the brightest moments and the darkest hours.

Judy McDowell, our lifelong friendship has been with me as we have grown together. Joey Schooley, your free and joyful spirit truly reminding me to laugh everyday. Cheryl Smelser for your beautiful heart and passion. Virginia Anderson and Christina Howe – Debbie's presence is still with us through our love and memories we share. My heartfelt gratitude goes out to all my sisters of the heart for your unending love and trust. I wish I could acknowledge you all individually.

Many thanks to my soul families in Florida, Toronto, B.C., Mt. Shasta, Iowa, Hawaii and in numerous places around the world.

Liah Howard – you were my first teacher. Your friendship and guidance were pivotal in helping me find my way on my new path.

Brian BecVar, Matisha, Shalomar, Lex Van Someren – your music and love inspires me to create.

Peggy Manning, thank you for providing me with a space to work, after helping to facilitate further healing in my heart. I love our work together.

Because of the number of years I have worked on this project, it is possible I might have left out the names of some special people who helped me along the way. If so, please accept my thanks and appreciation and know you are loved.

I am eternally grateful for the many hands and hearts that helped make this book possible. I love you all.

How blessed I am by the wisdom of Spirit and the Universe. I am always being taken care of and guided. Thank you God from the deepest part of my heart and soul for your constant presence and your abiding love.

I love you.

FOREWORD

Frannie's transformation from top model to spiritual intuitive didn't happen overnight. She had to face a debilitating illness, the pain and dysfunction of which forced her to look within and face her doubts and demons. The old external reinforcement – both financial and emotional – that she was used to in her modeling career disappeared. Indeed, her environmental illness made it necessary for her to walk around with an oxygen mask just to go outside. She was unable to work or function as a mother or as a wife. In a nutshell, she went from superwoman to cave-dweller almost overnight.

Forced to live in the world of her consciousness, Frannie began to look at thoughts and feelings she had always glossed over in her active worldly life catching planes to photo-shoots. She had to confront her fears head on and learn to walk with them. In this respect, her journey was indeed heroic and serves as a lodestone for others. Yet this is the archetypal journey we all take from darkness to light, from fear to love. It is a journey that means we often forfeit outside approval in order to be true to ourselves. It is a journey that pushes us to take emotional risks we had never thought of taking before.

When Frannie first talked to me about this book three or four years ago, I encouraged her to make a commitment to writing her story and I asked her to be as honest as she could about her challenges as well as her triumphs. "If you write only about the woman who connects with Jesus," I told her, "people will not see the depths of the transformation that happened in your life. They will make you special and feel that your story could never be theirs."

"The strength of your story," I told Frannie, "is not that it is special, but that it is the story of every person who leaves the world of name and fame to live a life guided by Spirit. For you, as for most people, it is not a life of worldly rewards, but of the rewards of the soul: ever-deepening love and friendship, authenticity, compassion and truth."

Those who live from the inside out rarely know what their lives are going to look like from year to year, month to month, or even day to day. They experience their lives as they unfold in unique ways and often expectedly. By paying attention to the inner significance of external events, they learn to stop reacting to the outside, to stabilize in their hearts, and to respond only when they are ready.

With less reactivity, life appears to slow down and can be lived and breathed in each moment. Space can be found in the mad pace of existence to commune with self and others, to center and assimilate experience, and to act in alignment with our deeper values and sense of purpose. And this, of course, is what spiritual practice is all about.

It is not enough to turn away from the world of form. Hiding from life is not an option. This is not the time of neo-monasticism or "new age" escapism.

This is a time of empowerment, a time when each one of us needs to begin looking within and taking responsibility for our thoughts, feelings and actions. This is the time when spirituality must be engaged in the warp and woof of daily existence, at home, at work, in our hearts and in our communities.

I know Frannie and I love her. Yes, she is a special person: radiant, loving, sincere. You would be happy to call her your friend, as I do. But she is not any more special than you are. Her journey from modeling clothes to modeling her essence is your journey and mine. All of us must drop our social masks and disguises if we want to touch the heart of truth.

It is a great journey that we take, not just once, but time and time again. We are all reaching for new masks and scaring each other silly until life shows us our foolishness and we have the courage to let the mask fall away.

In each moment, we are modeling something. Sometimes it is fear. Sometimes it is love. The question is not, "how can we get rid of our fear?" The question is "how can we hold our fear with love?"

The answer to that question can be found in these pages. And when you find it, you will feel its echo in your heart.

Blessings,

Paul Ferrini

There is a story that you are here to tell.
It is a story of a little girl
who begins to remember a part of herself, her true self.
This little girl then begins to share it with others
and then something stops her from sharing
and she stops to listen, she stops to feel and she stops to hear.

She hears silence. It is still.
She hears silence. It is soft.
She hears silence. It is delicious.

She waits for the voice to speak to her
and then one day in all her silence, she becomes the voice.
She begins to speak from the inside.
When she speaks, she is hearing at the same time.
It is all coming from one place within her being.
It just doesn't seem that important to talk anymore.
Yet when she does, it is because she is hearing at the same time.

She begins to move out into the world again
to share herself from this inner place.
It is her heart that is speaking and hearing at the same time.

Silent voice of Spirit, I am,
I have come to share my truth with you.
There is only one of us here experiencing as all mankind.
Let us join in the silence and voice our oneness
as love penetrates every part of existence.

The little girl is now all grown up.
She is still being the silence that wants to speak.
As she listens, she shares the truth with all she meets.

Book 1

Unfolding
the Myth

INTRODUCTION:
Unfolding the Myth

"Don't be satisfied with the stories that came before you.
Unfold your own myth." – Rumi

I came to Florida in 1989 to heal my body. I was suffering from chemical sensitivities so severe that I could no longer function and we hoped the cleaner environment would help. My body was experiencing acute symptoms and the fear that something was terribly wrong caused me constant distress. I soon realized my life had to change in every way to give myself a chance to heal.

This was the beginning of an inner journey for me and Englewood, Florida seemed like a safe place for me to get well. I was married at the time with two small children, Luke and Lane. My husband Bob and I decided we needed to make this move, so we packed up everything we owned and left our home in Toronto, Canada to start a new life. The healing of my body was my focus and it completely changed my life. Very quickly I realized that this new way of living consciously was beginning to open new doors, while at the same time beginning the process of closing old doors. Parts of me had to die so the true me could begin to really live.

Today, many of us are aware that we are Spiritual beings having a human experience. Knowing that, my greatest romance has been with God and with myself as a divine being. Every part of my life has helped me to know who I am. It is this dance with the dark and the light that has allowed me to meet myself. All of the negative aspects of myself that I have met and reacted to in others have brought me to more of me. This romance with myself has grown to be my truest love and I know now that wherever I am, that love and energy are always available for me.

My illness brought me deeper into the dark places of my shadow self. The demons within that place continued to create my life from fear. Fear that I was not worthy of the love and vast energy that is always around and within me. This love, that is truly our birthright, always seemed to be outside of me rather than inside of me. As my life challenged me to feel what was real, I began to realize that I couldn't be in love with the idea of love; I needed to be in love with me. In the past I was easily seduced away from myself. But as I detoxed and cleansed my sick body, all aspects of myself were touched and through this process I began to feel all my fears one by one. Often, I was so tired of fighting; I feared I would never feel well again. I was ready to leave this body, to walk away from this great gift of life. I wanted to die.

My teacher of love, Jesus, became the inspiration for my heart's healing. To me, he walked his talk. But my real heroes were the people in my day-to-day life. As we shared our journeys, we inspired and continue to inspire each other to live and persevere through life's challenges.

My sick body was simply the method God used to bring me face to face with the parts of me that were afraid to be all that I am. Through my chemical sensitivities, I learned how to say NO and to speak the truth of what I needed to feel. As I moved through the process of finding out who I am, I began to say, YES to life once again. I learned this world is not my enemy, but rather, the vehicle for love to move through me and to inspire me. My path is my own and the journey to God is the journey to self. Now when I breathe fully into this body, I give thanks for the opportunity to *be* the love that Jesus, Buddha, Mohammed, Baal Shem Tov, Krishna and Lao Tzu all modeled for us. Every moment of this life is a chance to shine the Christ Light. I do not have to wait for a special time or a special person, for in this very moment I can share it with the world.

It is important that I make the distinction here between Jesus Christ and the Christ Light, for they are not the same. The Christ Light is pure unconditional love. It is Universal energy, God's energy. This energy is not Jesus, though Jesus like all the Masters, did embody its essence. The Christ light is the light and energy of our true Source – the inner light that lives in each of us.

Every day I learn how to better accept my emotional body and not to react from that unconscious place of fear. I now know that my body is healed when my mind is healed. I am not afraid of death for my experiences have brought me to the clear knowledge that as soul I never die. The awareness that my fears need not define me has brought me to the simple truth that *I Am*. It has brought me the courage to be vulnerable and to live my life the way I choose to live it.

This life is ours to create. To live life to its absolute fullest is to live in love with self in every moment. We begin with our self and share the truth, whether it is our fear or our love. All that we have the courage to face within our self, will help bring us to the truth that we are searching for.

Getting to know myself has brought me deeper into my body so now I have the courage to walk authentically. For me, my true self is my God-self; the source of unconditional love that is our birthright. As human beings and spiritual beings, we really do not need illness to bring us back to our own heart. We do not need broken relationships to wake us up to our truth. We do not actually need these tragedies and dramas to shift us into feeling what is really going on inside. Yet this is all part of the way life works in the physical world. Life will provide us with whatever it takes to wake us up to the truth – and encourage us to make that shift. This is life and together we can know that every moment has brought us here to remember the truth – that we are all worthy of love. This love is our true nature and when we find it within ourselves we can step into our lives as open vessels for God's love to move through our hearts, healing us and touching others. We can look into the world outside of us and not be afraid of what we see. It is all to be experienced and embraced for our own learning and remembering.

God, Spirit, Angels, Jesus, the wind, my child, my friend, my sister, my brother, my ancestors, the trees, the silence and all creation speak words of inspiration within my heart. All I have to do is bring my attention to my body, to my heart. The words are all so simple as they move through my heart. These words, these feelings, these thoughts are in you as well, as you find yourself. The silence is longing to be touched by you. And in this space within, the light of love shines for all as you model the truth of self.

I invite you to read my love story. It is a story of the uncovering of the false self to find out that *I* am the love I have been searching for. The love of self is the greatest challenge and it takes deep commitment to know who we are not and in so doing discover who we truly are.

Love,
Frannie

1

Debbie's Death

*If you know who you are, then you have the courage to live
and you also have the courage to die.*

I did not know at the time how important the event of Debbie's death would be to my life. Do we ever really know at the time? Years later, I began to see the bigger picture. Debbie's death brought me to the greatest understanding of who I really am and my purpose for still being in my own body so I could share my story; and to share the part of Debbie's story that changed my life.

On August 25th, 1981, I received an urgent phone call. To my shock, I learned my close friend Debbie was dying. I had no details other than Debbie was in the hospital and on life support. I felt like I was in a dream; I was desperate to get to her.

I had never experienced anything like this. I drove home in a daze and cried for the entire one-hour drive to my hometown, Kitchener-Waterloo, Ontario. I went straight to her parents' home, but was distraught to learn when I got there that Debbie had died just before I arrived. An aneurysm had ruptured in her brain and her parents had made the wrenching decision to turn off the life support machines. I was too late to see her – to say goodbye to her. Her parents Marcey and Lorne were in shock and so was I.

Later, we went together to the funeral home to view Debbie's body before the public visitation. I needed to be near her again, to see her and to know that my love for her was greater than the grief that was choking me.

After seeing her daughter, Marcey said to me in despair, "Frannie, they made her look like an old lady. You know how she likes to look. Please, could you fix her?"

I did not hesitate. I heard Marcey's pain and I had to respond. I wanted to help, but I knew I was doing it for myself as well! I felt some other power guiding me because there was no doubt or fear when I said, "Yes, I will do it."

At this time in my life I was a very successful professional model. The day before Debbie's death I had been standing on a set shooting a futuristic commercial for Magnavox. I was the goddess of time, working with the actor Leonard Nimoy, Mr. Spock from *Star Trek*. The next day I was standing in a room with my girlfriend's dead body.

Now as I stood looking at her, I experienced a feeling of timelessness. It all felt like a dream. While going through the motions of fixing her hair, doing her make-up and polishing her nails, a greater power seemed to move through me. I talked to her as if she could hear me. I cried and shared my pain at her having left us. And through it all, I began to feel a love I had never felt before. I felt Debbie like never before. I could feel her right there in the room with me and I felt she was okay with all that had happened. Peace filled my heart. Debbie was not in her body anymore but I now felt her presence even stronger. Her soul was so alive in the room and in my heart that day, but I had no words at the time to express it. I did not know how to share the experience. How would anyone understand?

The week before, Debbie had been to a workshop focused on the work of Elizabeth Kubler-Ross, dealing with death and dying, and she was excited to share what she had learned. The workshop had been about embracing fears and Debbie's greatest fear was the fear of death. After the workshop, she had written a letter to all those she loved, sharing her healing from this fear. The day she died, she had dinner with her fiancée and her mother, and had just given the letter to her mother because she was off to a cottage for a holiday. The next moment the aneurysm burst in her head and Debbie fell to the floor unconscious. Hours later she was dead.

After the funeral I read that letter and was blown away by her insights into her fears. She wasn't afraid of death any more, she wrote. Many years later, I asked her mom if anyone kept the letter because now it would mean so much more to me. Marcey didn't know where it went, but she did tell me about the night before Debbie died. She said they were lying in bed holding each other and Debbie was sharing intimately and baring her soul. She shared, on a deeper level, about her dark side.

Debbie told her she believed God would speak to us at the end of our physical lives. For example, she felt God would say to the leader of our country (at the time), "Prime Minister Trudeau, I gave you a country, what did you do with it?" And God would do the same with us, "I gave you a life, what did you do with it?" Then Marcey shared with me that Debbie began to confess the parts of herself she didn't like. She told her mother she had lied a lot while she was growing up. They held each other while Debbie continued to share her dark secrets.

Marcey wept as she told me how much love she felt for her daughter that night. How could she have ever known that Debbie would die the next day?

Debbie discovered the truth of herself and in so doing, gave herself permission to die. My life is about finding the truth about myself because it enables me to live. Both are the same.

If you know who you are, then you have the courage to live and when the time comes, that same knowledge will give you the courage to die.

2

Feeling Debbie's Spirit

A few days before Debbie died, I thought I might be pregnant and over the phone I shared my secret with her. Since I was not sure, I went to the doctor and was awaiting the results of the blood test. I asked her not to tell anyone until I was sure.

During her funeral, many mutual friends came up and congratulated me on my pregnancy. I hadn't received the confirmation from the test results, but obviously Debbie was giving me the answer from Spirit through these friends - she always had difficulty keeping secrets. And she always had a sense of humor that I appreciated so much. Her laughter and zest for life, even with her many physical challenges, taught me so much about living in the moment.

When Debbie was young she had problems with her spine that caused her to walk with a slight limp and required her to wear braces on her legs and special shoes. As a result, she was always obsessed with her feet. They were very small and looked too tiny, even for her body - Debbie was only five feet tall. She constantly talked about her feet. She couldn't wait to get out of her orthopedic shoes. So when she was finally able to wear "normal" shoes, they had to be stylish... comfortable, but stylish.

May 17th, 1982 my son Lucas was born, eight months after Debbie's death. The nights I would get up to nurse or comfort our colicky baby boy, often I would feel Debbie's presence fill the room. As I sat rocking Luke in his room I would see her limping by the doorway. I would feel her standing there and as I would breathe into my fear of the possibility of her ghost visiting me, I would feel the same warmth and comfort I felt at the funeral home months before. When I would feel Debbie's spiritual presence, my body would be full of "truth chills" - that's what I called it when I got bumps all over. These visits from Debbie began with just a glimpse of her. It felt a bit like a dream, yet I could hear her communicating to me in this new way.

I don't know when those visitations stopped, but they did. It was most likely when I returned to modeling and was too busy to be still in a conscious way. There wasn't any quiet place within me for her to enter. I am more understanding of those times now and I am so grateful. Debbie was showing me another gift that I had. This gift was to feel and be aware of the presence of the non-physical world. To see, with my inner vision, the other planes of existence that are parallel to ours, to be on that bridge between the worlds. I didn't know it at the time, but I was being prepared for my work to come. I was very casual about these experiences, but kept them to myself, sharing them only with a few others. I didn't really understand what was going on. I still had doubts around the experiences. It was unfamiliar territory that I had no frame of reference for and I was focused on my new life as a mother.

Had Debbie known somewhere inside her she was about to die? Her new love of self, especially her dark side, which she had previously judged and feared, had opened her up to more of who she truly was. She had touched the false self so that the true self could live.

After Debbie's death my busy life did not feel as comfortable as it had before. My true spiritual self was calling for more and quietly, subconsciously, my journey back to self had begun. The busy outer world reflected my inner pain and slowly, gradually, I began to feel the dis-ease of my body.

3

When the Student Is Ready,
the Teacher Appears

Our daughter Lane was due February 14th, 1985, but on December 1st, I went into premature labor during my girlfriend's wedding. By the time I got to the nearest hospital, I was already dilated. The doctor in the small town of St. Catharines, Ontario, looked like the detective from the television series, *Colombo*. He walked into the emergency room in his full-length trench coat and messed up hair and said he was going to put me upside down so the baby wouldn't come out. I couldn't believe what I was hearing, but I was in so much fear I would try anything as long as my baby would be okay. It was amazing to experience this old fashioned way but it sure beat chemicals.

The next morning I went by ambulance to the old Women's College Street Hospital in Toronto, where my own doctor met me. The ultrasound showed the baby's head was crowned and ready to come any time. They said they would do everything possible to delay the delivery, but I was afraid that the baby would not survive. I prayed for a miracle.

This was a teaching hospital, so there were always a lot of interns and nurses looking at me. That night, a female East Indian doctor came in to examine me. This woman said so calmly to me, "What will stop this baby from coming, is you. There is a full moon tonight and you can tell your baby to move its head to the opposite direction. The baby will hear you. The power and the energy of the moon are high in vibration tonight. You can change your situation. Your baby will hear you."

I was completely intrigued. I had no real understanding of what she was saying but I was totally open and ready to do anything, so I believed her. I began to pray and then talked to my baby just as she had told me to. Soon, my stomach began to move like there was something rocking the waters within. My baby was moving as if there was a power inside changing her position. I tapped into this power within me. I knew the baby was listening. The interns on call that night all began watching. It was very exciting and there was so much love present. In all, my stomach was a rockin' and rollin' for a couple of hours! When it finally settled down and was calm again, I knew my baby was okay. There was a profound sense of peace in me and I just knew that everything was going to be fine.

The ultrasound the next morning confirmed what I already knew. During the experience the night before, the baby had turned and now her head was beneath my heart and her legs were cross-legged over my cervix. It seemed like a miracle! This was a life-changing experience for me. Lane was one determined little baby.

Throughout my stay in the hospital I went into labor many times, but by taking medications and talking to Lane, I helped her to wait. After almost two months in the hospital, our little girl, Lane Frances arrived on January 22, 1985.

Baby Lane had listened – and I believed in the miracle. I had faith, for that night the East Indian doctor had shared a higher truth with me. I was ready to believe in another way of living; to believe in myself and my ability to connect with my higher power. My heart was calling for the truth and my baby could hear me. Because I was ready to share my fear, my cry for help was heard. God listened to my prayer and sent a messenger. I was ready to live the truth I had experienced. When the student is ready, the teacher appears.

4

My Birth (An Act of Faith)

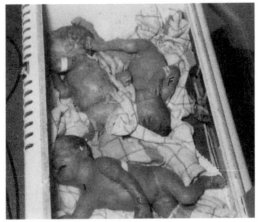

I came into this world with two "womb-mates." I am a triplet. Colleen is my identical twin and Philomene is our fraternal sister. At birth we each weighed only three pounds and afterward went down to a pound or less. But our mother believed in miracles and a miracle is what it took for us to survive.

Mom tells a beautiful story about our birth. It's fun to watch her tell it because my dad often interrupts her with his version.

Before we were born, our mother had a stillborn baby. She knew inside something was wrong, yet her doctor assured her she was okay, even though he knew the baby was dead. He wanted my mother to abort the baby naturally. She carried the baby a few more weeks, but when she went into labor and the child was delivered, the umbilical cord was wrapped around the baby's neck. I guess it had died slowly inside of her. (How blessed I was during the birth of my babies to have such advanced technology with monitors and ultrasound.)

This death was devastating for my parents. The baby boy was full size and there was nothing wrong with him in any other way. My parents had a funeral for him but the priest would not bless the grave because the baby was dead at the birth. I believe this experience shattered my father's faith in the Church because he did not get the support he needed at this traumatic time.

My mom has Rh-negative blood and my dad has Rh-positive blood. This combination often creates serious complications for both the mother and baby. If the baby's blood is introduced to the mother's system, it can trigger an attack response from the mother as if the baby were an invading foreign body .

My mother had previously had many miscarriages. Between her history and the mixing of the blood types, any pregnancy was considered high-risk. The doctors had told her after the death of the baby in utero that she would have problems conceiving and carrying full term. Even though this news broke her heart, my mom had incredible faith and she still felt her purpose here on earth was to have babies. It was her greatest desire.

After this news, dad took mom to Quebec for a vacation. There is a sacred place called St. Joseph's Oratory where people go for healing. As my parents climbed the stairs to the top of the hill to the chapel, they saw crutches and wheelchairs dropped and discarded along the way where the crippled and diseased had been healed. My mom decided she would pray for a miracle. Just before she knelt on the step, she closed her eyes and consciously decided what she wanted. She prayed for twins. It is a long-standing joke that my mom prayed for twins and that my dad threw in an extra prayer. That night we were conceived.

My mother taught me about faith. She believed in a higher power, so even though she was told she would never be pregnant again, she did not accept it. My mother knew what she wanted and with God's help, it happened. We were born exactly eleven months to the day after my brother died. We all had Rh+ blood like our dad but miraculously there were no complications. Then another miracle happened. Our healthy brother Philip was born a year and a half later. My parents then had four babies – all in diapers!

5

Wellness Through Our Illness

About three months after Lane was born, I went back to my modeling career. Like most mothers with a new baby, I was tired all the time. So every morning I would put on make-up to cover up the truth of what was really going on. I was still very busy in my career, for which I was grateful. My husband was building his renovation business and it was flourishing. I was trying to do it all, to be a mother, a wife and a career woman. Superwoman.

We were living in a brand new house we had built. My energy levels just kept getting steadily lower. Pretty soon, I was sick all of the time. To compensate, I just got busier and busier so that I could not hear the conflicts going on inside of me. We had hired a nanny, Clare, from the Philippines. She moved in to help with Luke and Lane and instantly became family.

One day I got a flu that knocked me down. I was so sick that I could barely get out of bed. My agent called to say that I was to leave for the Bahamas in a few days for two weeks of shooting for the Tourist Board. It was a wonderful job, the kind every model wants, but I could not even imagine getting on a plane to go and work. Still, I accepted the job.

Then Clare came in and told me she had some antibiotics. I can't believe I took them but I did. I wanted the quick fix. At this point in my life I was not conscious of taking care of my body and I lived in constant denial with what was really going on. I was on the merry-go-round of life and I did not have the frame of reference to think about the outcome.

I took the pill without even knowing what it was and went to sleep. When I woke up I could barely walk to the bathroom. I felt so drugged and lost in the feelings of my physical body. The next day, I drove to talk with the clients I was traveling to the Bahamas with and while I was driving I was outside my body looking down at myself in the car. This was my first conscious out-of-body experience and it scared me.

I went on the trip and that drained whatever juice I had left right out of me.   When I arrived back in Toronto, I felt very vulnerable and unhappy with my life. I was still looking for comfort outside of myself. I wanted my husband's attention but he was very busy with his business. I felt completely lost and I cried a lot. I became sicker and sicker and I could not understand what was happening to me. I used to be such a happy person, or so I thought.

I continued working every day. Then one day, as I was modeling a designer's new collection, I began to feel sick. I felt drugged and disoriented. My words started to slur. What little energy I had, plummeted. I wanted to curl up in the corner and go to sleep. I managed to get through the day and somehow I drove home. When I got there, I went into the house and just sat alone in a corner and rocked as I stared at the wall.

Unbeknownst to me and to everyone around me, I was having one of my first severe reactions to chemicals. My children and nanny saw me in this state and did not know what to do. I had no idea what was happening. Inside I was calling for help, but on the outside I was unable to speak or to move. Apparently I looked like the people I had seen in movies in mental institutions who just sat rocking and staring into space. Inside I was so afraid.

After some hours my motor activities gradually came back and I went to bed with flu-like symptoms. My skin was yellow, and my eyes were glassy. Sounds felt incredibly loud to me; my nerves were raw. As tired as I was, I was unable to sleep. I felt wired like I drank too much coffee. This was the first of many reactions. I was terrified – and so were my husband and family.

Here I was in 1987, a 34-year-old mother of two and I felt like I was dying in a dark hole of fear. My body was so weak and vulnerable that any breath of a chemical pollutant would put me in a catatonic state for hours. Unable to connect my will with my body, I simply left it. I left myself. I'd stare for hours without blinking, unable to speak or move my body on my own.

Sometimes it would be a gradual reaction, as all my motor activities would slow down. At the beginning fear would take over because it was an unknown place and I was afraid I would die. For days afterward, I would not be able to function very well. My body was poisoned and the flu-like symptoms would overwhelm me for days. The nausea, body aches, headaches or migraines, swelling of the joints and low energy would keep me in bed.

Between reactions I searched for answers. I went to a medical doctor who told me he'd take a CAT scan and if it did not reveal anything, he'd put me on tranquilizers. The test showed nothing and as he looked at me without compassion and began writing a prescription, I heard a voice inside of me screaming to leave and never come back. It was as if there was a force guiding me in that moment that was greater than my sickness.

That voice saved my life. Somehow, somewhere deep inside I knew that voice was my true spiritual self moving me into a greater truth. In that moment I believed I would die if I didn't get out of there. Maybe that was the first time in my life I had truly loved myself enough to do what I needed to do for me. From that moment on I was conscious of being guided and I listened.

My prayer for help was heard because within days my sister-in-law Paulette, who was a nurse, shared with me some information about the formaldehyde in new kitchen cupboards, which could make people sick. Then my sister Philomene began to learn about homeopathic medicine and holistic healing. I was open. I knew I was dying and I had to find another way to live in my body and in this world. My body was so toxic; I had run out of options.

From then on, everything that came my way became a stepping-stone to knowing my truth. There was not much space inside of me – my cup was full and every breath was vital. I needed pure air, pure food and pure love. I was hearing my own cry for help. There was no place to go but inside – to get in touch with myself as soul.

6

Entering Inside

Chemical sensitivities was the illness and it became the gift to my own healing. I find it interesting that I created this sickness as a vehicle to transport me from the outer world to the great beauty of my inner world. The outer world was a reflection of my old self. I used it to identify and validate myself in its image of me. And the gift of EI (Environmental Illness) internalized the outer world, making it toxic to my physical body. The material, three-dimensional world, which had defined me, became the catalyst that ultimately brought me into my true self.

EI, or chemical sensitivities, is an immune system breakdown. Because of a weakened immune system, I had become sensitive to many things in the environment around me. Every breath of air, free of the world's common toxins, became vital for me. One inhalation of impure air – perfume, fragrance, cleaning solvents, or any chemical out-gassing from such common items as cars, carpets, house paint, or many building materials used in modern homes, could throw me into a catatonic state. My mind would cease to function clearly and the connection between my brain and motor abilities would begin to slow down. It felt as if all my bodily functions were starting to shut down. I could not relate or comprehend clearly and I spoke and moved as if drugged.

I was losing control and felt helpless in my situation. For example, I would stare at walls for hours, my eyes dilated in a drug-like stupor. The simple action of lifting my hand to my face was too difficult. It just wouldn't work. My mind and my nervous system seemed totally disconnected. The toxins caused swelling in my brain or at least that's how it felt. My heart beat more rapidly and all these feelings were extremely uncomfortable and frightening. Yet it was feeling these physical symptoms that brought me back to my body, myself. I was no longer able to play all the roles I had created in my life, which kept me focused on everyone but me.

Every day I was vulnerable and sick. The confidence I once had, which was totally dependent on external validation, was stripped away all at once. I had no energy to give to myself, much less any for my husband Bob, our son Luke who was now four years old and two-year-old Lane. My body felt naked, weak and dying. Daily I struggled with every task, every action. At times I could not go out into the world without an oxygen tank, or a mask and still the pollution would invade my body through my skin. Every breath of pure air was vital to my recovery. It felt terrible to be so sensitive, feeling like I had no control over the next moment. I had to do what I needed to do to feel safe.

The foods I ate were also very important. I was tested for allergies and food sensitivities, which encouraged me to become a vegetarian and to eat only organically grown foods. I learned that certain foods caused my body to react and that by balancing my diet I could reduce the stress on it.

Changing my life was a drastic experience. I had to separate myself from the world I had previously been so much a part of and identified with. I became, in effect, "organically grown." Contrary to everything required of me in my work as a model, I had to move away from my external concerns of appearance, as my inner world of truth became more and more important.

Bob was working out of town building his dream house and was not able to be there for me emotionally. As a result, it was necessary for me to give myself what I needed on the inside. I did not understand at the time that Bob's emotional absence was allowing me to move closer to my truth. I could no longer depend on his validation to fill the void inside me. Bob was doing what he needed to do to take care of himself and his family the best way he knew how.

Philomene came to live with us to help me with Luke and Lane while I was searching for answers. One day she brought home a book called *Creative Visualization* by Shakti Gawain. I was fascinated with the words of inspiration, which guided me to my own silence and peace.

When Philomene came home from her teaching job where she taught music to elementary school children, she would take over for me so I could take care of myself. I would then go and sit in a bath, or meditate in my room – alone with myself. My other sister Colleen was totally empathic to my sickness. Without going through the same illness, she was able to feel me and helped create a safe place for me to heal. She seemed to always be conscious of my needs even when I was too sick to care about myself. Colleen and Philomene took over for me in the areas of my life where I had no energy. My father went to the library and got books on healing for me. He also drove me to my doctor's appointments when I was too weak to go alone. My mother created menus so I could have new recipes to cook with. I would often call her and cry and share all of my feelings and she was able to listen without judgment. It was all so very overwhelming for me yet with the help of my family I felt supported.

My brother Philip, whose presence speaks directly into my heart, is a loving constant in my life. He gave me the books that continue to inspire me to this day – the *I Ching* by R.L. Wing and *The Little Book Of The Tao Te Ching* by John R. Mabry. The Chinese have long understood that every aspect of life is constantly in a state of change. At any given moment our life can show us aspects of ourselves – that which is falling away and that which is taking shape. We are leaving behind parts of self that no longer serve us as we acquire new depths of awareness about who we are and who we are becoming.

My brother Phil has learned to bring his inner self into the world through his films. His gift of silence, expressing himself in ways other than words, became a gentle reminder for me to go inside to connect with my true spiritual self. These words of the Tao remind me of my brother and I am grateful for his way of teaching me and all those he touches. He helped me find a part of myself I didn't know until I chose to go inside to my own silence.

The Little Book Of The Tao Te Ching by John R. Mabry
The softest thing in the world
Overcomes the hardest thing in the world.
That which is without substance can enter
Even where there is no space.
Therefore I know the value of non-action.
Teaching without words
And benefit without actions.
There are few in the world who can grasp it.[1]

The more I unplugged from the world and gave myself this quiet time, the more I wanted. I loved the experience within. This new connection with Spirit was the answer to my soul's longing. I became committed to this experience throughout the day. There, I found a peace I hadn't known for a very long time. This gave me the hope and the courage to embrace my illness. New doors were opening. I found books and I was given so much help.

This is when I met a homeopathic doctor named Fernando Ania. He looked into my eyes and said, "I will help you," and I trusted him right away. He listened to my symptoms. He asked questions. He wanted to know me. I spilled out all of my pain and cried, "I don't know what to do. I feel as if I'm going crazy. I feel like I'm insane."

I believe this was the breaking point in my life. I could no longer live the life I had been living before. I was denying my soul's truth. I knew deep down there had to be another way to find my health, my love and my life. Doctor Fernando Ania became my friend. He took my hand and led me to the part of myself that was calling to be heard. He believed I would get well and he helped me understand a new way of treating disease. I asked my friend Dawn Quiacos, who graduated from Fernando's School of Homeopathy in Ontario, to give me her description of this type of health care. This is what she wrote:

Homeopathy:

Samuel Hahnemann was a German physician in the early 1800's. Exemplifying a theory going back to Socratic times, Hahnemann observed that cure arises when the disease is met with similar forces. Literally translated, homeopathy means 'similar suffering': a medicine that produces a totality of symptoms in the healthy cures that same totality of symptoms in the sick.

Homeopathy made its introduction to North America in the 1900's. Homeopathic medicine is more commonly known for its lack of side effects and its effectiveness in treating acute illnesses such as fever or the common cold. It is becoming recognized as a complement to allopathic medicine with its use, for example, in expediting post-surgical healing, alleviating the side effects of pharmaceutical drugs and for those with long-standing, chronic situations when other actions are not met with complete success.

More importantly, however, homeopathy does not simply treat the illness. Homeopathic medicine prescribes on a totality of symptoms: physical, mental/emotional and spiritual. We become more in touch with ourselves and our surroundings and more aware of our actions and their effects.

I began taking remedies based on my symptoms and my constitution. The symptoms from my past began to show their face again. My healing was beginning and I was going deeper within myself, unlocking sicknesses that had been trapped within me for years. I can't say that I felt better; I did not. I felt like I was slipping away into a darker hole. But Fernando believed that I would get well and in this belief, he held the space for my wellness.

We finally realized that our brand new house was contributing to my sickness. Many of the new building materials and products were out-gassing and poisoning me. Bob was a renovator. He began to do what he could to support me here through my illness.

He found another older home and began to make it a healthy house for me to live in, a place where I continued to heal. He took out the carpets and put in tile and hardwood floors. There was nothing new gassing out like appliances, carpet, or furniture.

In addition to chemical sensitivities, I was also diagnosed with candida albicans – a yeast overgrowth. Like many people in North America, I unknowingly suffered from the many different symptoms and physical discomforts of candida. Previously, I was treated for a number of allergies and poor digestion. I was given antibiotics, birth control pills, hormones and other drugs. Still, I felt overtired, overstressed and over worked. For me this new diagnosis was a huge eye-opener because I was definitely affected by an overabundance of yeast. I was not in balance in my gut and this imbalance resulted from my dis-ease. (For more information about candida, check out the *Complete Candida Yeast Guidebook* by Jeanne Marie Martin with Zoltan Rona, M.D.)

We each have the ability to actively participate in the health of our bodies by understanding the way the body works and educating ourselves. We can help the healing process by taking responsibility for our health into our own hands; by consciously choosing to bring ourselves back into balance – physically, mentally and emotionally.

Each day was a struggle to be in my body. Some days I wanted to die, to free myself from the pain of living. But the more I opened to my inner self, the more I began to feel the presence of Spirit, a sense of God. I was beginning to feel whisperings of love inside me. But I also felt the darkness. It is very difficult for me now to admit that I lost my desire to be a mother and a wife. My responsibilities seemed too many, the demands of my external world too hard.

I needed my energy to restore a healthy balance to my physical body. I started to cleanse it of poisons and toxins such as preservatives, pesticides, chemicals, air pollutants, heavy metals and many other substances. Cleansing treatments benefited me greatly because reducing harmful contaminants in the body helped me rebuild my weakened immune system. The immune system is our body's natural defense system against disease.

In addition, my diet and other stresses in my life had created an acidic constitution. Robert O. Young, PhD and Shelley Redford Young, in their book, *The pH Miracle*, show that there is a direct correlation between overacidification of body fluids and tissues, and both disease and "dis-ease." They explain that illnesses and their symptoms are warnings from our bodies that optimal pH levels are out of balance; and that good health is restored when acid/base (pH) balance is maintained through diet.

Growing up, my father had a meat plant and I'd guess eighty percent of my food intake was protein, which is very acidic. I probably ate enough meat for ten lifetimes! Vegetables were frozen or canned. Living food was not a big part of any meal. It was just the way back then.

Nowadays the high protein myth still persists and is taking a toll on our bodies. Dr. Ted Morter, in his book *Your Health Your Choice*, warns that too much protein puts a tremendous stress on the body. So much so that our natural healing process is sabotaged, leaving us vulnerable to the many chronic diseases which are becoming all too common.

My diet became healthier as I eliminated any foods that were stressing my body. I was now juicing and eating foods that were more alkaline, like green vegetables, to bring my body into balance.

Choosing to create health takes true commitment to a lifestyle that supports me. Holistic healing for me is about using natural remedies and treatments, eating wholesome foods, exercising, breathing clean air and drinking clean water. Over the last fifteen years, I have learned to make healthy foods that taste really good and I've explored and experimented with many healing modalities that seemed beneficial for me. I had to go back to the school of life and become more educated about my body.

Each day, all of my energy was required to prepare the right foods, to juice, to detoxify, to feel my pain and my hurts and to

just get through the day. I became very self-absorbed and separated
from the outer world. The only connection I desired was with
God, because there was no effort in that space of peace. I was
being fed by the truth I was so hungry for. Gradually, I began
feeling that I couldn't love anyone or anything outside myself. I
had so many mixed emotions. Guilt and shame consumed me.

I was letting go of patterns I learned as a child. I was learning
how to say "no," and to take care of my own needs. I was hungry
for truth and I was hungry for food that would nourish my body
and heal it. God sent me beautiful teachers, healers and books to
help me.

When I began to meditate, my mind was cluttered with
unwanted thoughts. I now realize meditation allowed those
thoughts to move through and then out of my unconscious. I
began to journal, which helped to process my thoughts and feelings.
I began to embrace my emotional body without judgment. Poetry
filled the blank pages of my book and I was surprised at the creative
writings that danced across the pages. I began to understand how
important the written words were for me. I grew more and more
in touch with my feelings. This was a safe place for me to express
all the hurt, the pain, the joy and the peace. The inner world was
calling for my attention even more strongly.

My new way of life was dramatically different from my past.
Healing was my priority and I was committed to it. Every chance
I could, I would meditate. I did everything possible to detoxify.
When I found out I had candida, I went on a strict diet that helped
me get that condition under control and my body back in balance.
The books *Fit For Life* and *Fit For Life 2*, by Harvey and Marilyn
Diamond, became my bibles.

With the understanding that my body needed to detoxify and
to re-build in a more balanced way, I changed my way of feeding
myself. As Harvey says, I started "eating to live instead of living to
eat." Information about natural hygiene opened my eyes to the
fact that my body naturally knew what to do. It was screaming

with pain to be heard. This quote from Harvey Diamond is worth remembering:

> "*All the nutritional requirements that the human body has – all carbohydrates and fatty acids that exist, that the human body needs to survive – are found in fruits and vegetables. The nutritional requirements are carried by the water in those fruits and vegetables into your intestines, where all nutrition is absorbed.*"[2]

It seems as if most of North America eats to pollute the body instead of cleanse it. We shower our outside body with water, why should we not clean ourselves inside?

I was born constipated and like many North Americans, throughout my youth my body became a waste dump of undigested material that had putrefied and fermented in my stomach, intestines and colon, resulting in an acidic constitution. So much energy was wasted in digesting. The mass of spoiled, rotted food produced alcohol in the digestive tract, which had the same consequences as drinking alcohol. I would feel as if I had a constant hangover.

From these books I learned how to combine food properly for the natural body cycles of digestion, absorption and elimination. I had more energy to rebuild by eating more living food like raw vegetables and fruits, which are high water content foods. My body cells could now actually receive nutrients and the water in the food would carry off toxic waste.

There is so much information in these books that truly helped save my life. One remarkable aid I found very effective is the use of castor oil packs. This therapy can be traced back to the work of Edgar Cayce, who is considered by many to be a twentieth century mystic. He was best known for the information he received while he was in a self-induced sleep state. By lying down, closing his eyes and folding his hands over his stomach, the sleeping Cayce brought in messages from spiritual guides on the inner worlds, for everything from the components of a well-balanced diet to how to overcome life-threatening illnesses.

In his book, *Beyond Theory. Edgar Cayce's Natural Health*, author Phil Thomas states:

"A healthy body begins with the ability to eliminate properly and one of the primary tools for assisting this is the castor oil pack. To use the pack, a minimal amount of castor oil is placed on a piece of quilted cotton or wool flannel that is inside a plastic bag with one side, which rests against the skin, partially cut away. I use an ice bag that is filled with hot water and positioned on top of the cloth. You may prefer another heat source. The heat drives the oil into the body during the course of say a one-hour session. As the oil penetrates the body it lubricates the region, assisting in the evacuation of the large intestine and therefore promoting lymph drainage. Cayce usually recommended using the pack over the right side of the abdomen sometimes to enhance function of the ileocecal valve, the sphincter valve connecting the small and large intestines, or perhaps a little higher up to assist in flushing the liver and gall duct. Of course the pack can enhance lubrication and drainage in many parts of the body, as well as reduce pain. However, there are places where one would generally not use it. As an example, you would not use a castor oil pack over the cranial region or over the heart."[3]

The use of colonics was also something that aided me in my detox. I was introduced to this healing modality and led to Alain Menard who had been doing colonics for over twenty years. He told me that colonic cleansings are the easiest way to clean the colon and rid the body of toxins. It's a gentle process that sends water into the colon, which will soften and remove the old undigested matter, mucous and toxins out of the body. By doing so, the body can rejuvenate and return to its original state of health and well being.

The whole idea of having someone put a tube up your rectum and stand there to help with the process is intimidating. Yet I felt so at ease because of this man's gentle nature and the unconditional love that he shares. This service is really just the store front for all the healing love and gifts of wisdom he offers. Every time I detoxed in this way I felt comfortable and grateful. At the beginning I had to go weekly for about six weeks. Soon my colon started to work more efficiently and slowly but surely my physical symptoms lessened.

As I began incorporating into my life all I had read and all I had learned, I became clearer in my mind and had more energy for day-to-day life. However, there were still some days I simply didn't want to live. I was tired of the emotional and physical pain and all the effort. At those times it was more difficult to quiet my mind. I wanted to crawl into a dark hole and disappear. Depression became a real challenge. I remembered how my mother would slip into despair when depression overtook her life. Now I knew how she felt.

Yet, somewhere deep inside I knew the depression was actually serving me by forcing me deep within to face my shadow self, to find out who I was, who I really am. Somewhere deep inside my heart and mind, I knew I was getting well. When my body felt better I would have the energy to cope with the stresses that were in my life.

With my strong connection to Spirit and the new feeling of wellness in my physical body, I began to believe there was a purpose for me to be here on the planet. I had the strength to go inside and listen to my heart and choose to live in this body in another way. I began to teach this way of eating in the meditation classes I now facilitated.

In 1993 I had the privilege of meeting Harvey Diamond in Sarasota, Florida and our hearts connected. His friendship is a bright light in my life. His books changed my life. I encourage you to read these books to see for yourself and to open your mind to food combining. We truly are what we eat and what we think. When I chose to live in this body fully, many teachers – both people and books – touched my life to bring me healing of body, mind and Spirit.

7

Finding Home

When I first got sick, my illness overpowered me. I had to face the truth that I could not model anymore. I was too sick and the environment of the workplace was not a safe place for me to be, let alone to get well. The industry was toxic for my vulnerable body. I was learning that even wearing new clothing was poisoning me. New clothing has formaldehyde in the fabric and with all of the synthetic material, make-up, hair spray, all kinds of fragrances, studio fumes from paints and chemicals, the industry was not helping me to get better. I was very weak and losing weight every day.

There were rumors going around in the business that I had AIDS. I guess the symptoms were similar because it also had to do with the immune system. I did not have AIDS, but I did have the so-called "20th Century Disease" – a very severe case of it and no one knew very much about chemical sensitivities at the time.

I believe that most of us on the planet have sensitivities and allergies because of the buildup of toxins in our bodies from chemicals in foods and the products of the material world we live in. We do not have enough fresh air to breathe, or clean water to drink. I also believe that my body had been crying out for help since I was a little girl because I always got sick so easily.

Now I know we do not have to wait until our bodies break down with disease. We can be present and aware now to the symptoms that tell us we need to detoxify. The information is all now easily available. We don't have to wait until our bodies get as sick as mine did or wait until our bodies are filled with cancer or our hearts stop working. My illness made me aware and conscious of what I was feeding it and the importance of pure air and an oxygenated body.

With the encouragement of my homeopathic and naturopathic doctors, I moved with my family to Englewood, Florida, on the Gulf of Mexico. Starting our new life here and not knowing anyone did not bother me in the least. I was excited for the adventure of re-uniting with the souls that were waiting to meet us again in this life.

The first day of school we met the Eason family at the bus stop. Gail and her children J.P. and Amanda were there to greet us. There was an instant connection for us all. Luke and J.P. are still best friends to this day. Gail was searching on her spiritual path as was I, and with the help of her father we were introduced to many inspiring books like *What Do You Really Want For Your Children?* and *Your Erroneous Zones*, by Wayne Dyer. His messages guided us in raising our children as they opened us up to another way to live our lives. Gail and Phil Eason have been extended parents for Luke and Lane as they grew up in Englewood and a blessing in my life. Meeting them helped me to feel at home in a town where I knew no one.

At the time, I used an oxygen tank to help me get some relief when I traveled in a car or on an airplane. It also helped me a great deal when I had to go out into the world for things like groceries. As well, I often had to humble myself to wear a mask when I went into public. I would still feel sick after being out in the world because my pores would breathe even though my nostrils were covered up. The skin is the largest organ of the body and I learned my pores were breathing in the toxins as well. Oxygen. I needed oxygen!

The home we bought was on the Bay right across the street from the ocean. Here I found my sacred healing place; the water and the sandy beach and the pure salt air. We were far away from industry and I felt safe to breathe fully and enjoy the natural fragrances of the many flowering trees and bushes. I was so grateful to be able to breathe fully again. Our property had a great many oak trees and the birds were abundant. I felt like I had found my heaven on earth.

It is quite wonderful to realize now that I created a physical illness in which everything made me truly feel and become more aware of myself and my body and everything around me. Here, I felt safe - and I was so grateful. God was guiding me and taking me home to my heart. Yet, at times it was unbearable to live through because I felt everything so intensely. I couldn't do anything without thinking about it. I couldn't take anything for granted. Every breath was vital to my survival. Everything on the physical level was challenged and I was learning to take care of myself and find out who my authentic self was. This is where I began learning about my breath.

There is one basic truth worth looking at here - THERE IS NO LIFE WITHOUT BREATH. Because like our heartbeat, our breathing is an autonomic function of the human body, most of us take it for granted. I began to realize that when I was in a reaction in my physical body, or when I was in fear, I wasn't breathing properly. So I began to be aware of my breath consciously and when I did, it would calm me. When I was in pain and my breath was only in my chest, I would consciously bring my awareness to my belly and breathe deeper. As I centered myself, I would feel more present. I needed my own breath.

Even though it is an automatic biological function, breath, when used consciously, can bring more health to your body. Your breath is the connection between your body and your mind.

There are all kinds of breathing techniques and schools of thought around breathing. Breath can be used to reduce stress, increase your energy and heighten your self-awareness, heal emotional wounds and traumas and help connect you more fully with Spirit. Your breath helps you to clean toxins out of your system and release physical symptoms caused by conditions of the mental and emotional body.

Your breath can help you resolve old, repressed feelings that are vibrating at a lower frequency in your electromagnetic field. And I find that mentally, my conscious breath can clear 'old tapes.'

Getting rid of these out-of-date thought forms brings me new peace and clarity. That's one reason why I love to meditate or just be mindful of my breath, for it connects me to my higher self. I read once in Gaia Budhai's flyer (Synergy Yoga of Ft. Lauderdale, FL): *To the degree that the breath is open and flowing, we are in the flow of life.*

8

Hello My Wondrous Friends

I found myself on a Spiritual path that was bringing me peace and comfort. I was reading inspiring books that seemed to answer the multitude of questions in my heart. The fresh sea air of the Gulf of Mexico provided me with the healing sanctuary I needed for my sick body. It was during this time of learning and quiet healing that Judy, my girlfriend from the time I was fifteen years old, came to visit me in my new home. I was very excited to see my childhood friend and share all that was happening in my life and all that was feeding my soul.

Judy was going through a relationship breakup and she was feeling a lot of her wounds. I found it easy to be compassionate towards her pain because of the work I was doing with my own past emotional wounds. She was very eager to meditate with me.

Early in her visit, we went into my bedroom and sat on the floor by my altar. To prepare ourselves, we sat in silence. Soon, words began to come through me that guided us both to an inner place where we felt safe and loved within ourselves. It wasn't that I no longer felt myself still in the room with her, but rather I felt I had expanded into an amazing vastness within me. I felt bigger. A vast river of love and energy had begun flowing through me. I felt as if I was standing outside of my body looking at myself, while at the same time my body and my life were a little speck in this huge energy I was also a part of.

Suddenly, I felt an energy enter me that wanted to speak. At the same time I felt my own resistance because I did not understand what was happening. One phrase just kept going through my mind over and over again until I just surrendered and opened myself up. The energy kept building until finally the voice burst out through me, "Hello my wondrous friends!" As I allowed the words to come through, I began seeing visions; at the same time I had an intrinsic understanding at other levels within myself, of what was going on.

It is easier to share this experience all these years later, because ever since that pivotal day, it has been one of the most important parts of my life. When I came back into my body and opened my eyes, there was Judy, sitting with her mouth open. "What was that?" she asked in stunned amazement. I was afraid, yet I was also filled with an incredible sense of peace and calmness. Judy reported she had been sitting peacefully in the meditation state, when I began to allow the new energy and vibration to move through my voice. The hurt and pain she was feeling in her heart seemed to be the target of all of this energy. It moved right into her heart with great intensity and then she felt herself opening to the love and wisdom being shared with us.

Judy was staying for a week, so we were eager to repeat the experience and maybe ask some questions. In actual fact, I didn't think it would happen again, but I certainly wanted to find out more. The next time we sat to meditate, I was filled with doubts and fears. Still, I felt compelled to proceed. We had both experienced so much healing and peace in the presence, that we wanted to experience it again.

We waited patiently in the silence as I opened myself to the energy. I had been doing automatic writing, asking my higher-self questions and receiving answers, so I simply sat in the same way while inviting this experience to show itself again.

Sure enough, I soon began to feel the same strong presence near me and then in this expanded state, the voice once again spoke, "Hello, my wondrous friends!" Judy welcomed the entity and began to ask questions. While the words were flowing through me, I was able to see and know more than the actual words were expressing and my heart began to overflow with happiness and great joy. It felt as if a long time friend I hadn't seen for years had just showed up on my doorstep.

The entity said his name was Remos and he identified himself as my Spirit guide. In my third eye, I began seeing another lifetime where he had been my teacher. When the communication was over, I came back into my body fully conscious of what had happened and what had been said, but it all seemed like a dream.

Through the week we repeated our meditation every day and we pieced a lot of information together about the lifetime Remos and I had shared. As I continued to write or speak the words that moved through me, I felt a very strong connection to this guide and continued to feel his presence throughout the days to come. Still, I questioned and doubted the experience every day. Yet going to that place of silence and merging with the energy showed me so much. It was a great comfort at this time in my life. Each day I spent a few hours allowing, indeed inviting this communication and connection to happen. It brought wisdom and knowledge that was helping me find my way back to my life in this body.

I believe that Judy's safe friendship was the energy that allowed me to begin this new and exciting part of my life. To share the gift with another is what brings the most love. I always say now I cannot experience this gift without another to share it with.

The day came for Judy to return home to Canada. One last time we sat in meditation together. During this last session, I heard the words, "You are going to get a flat tire." Immediately I went to Bob and shared this warning. Since I had a long drive to the airport and needed to get Judy there on time, he suggested I take his truck because he had just put new tires on it that week. Great! Listening to this guidance was fun. Safe now in Bob's truck, we were on our way to the airport sharing all of the excitement and happenings of the week, including our experiences with Remos. Suddenly the truck began making a weird noise. Sure enough, we had a flat tire! I had been given information and guidance and for me that flat tire was confirmation that what I had been receiving was truth.

This was a beginning for me to welcome the Spiritual guide into my life. I do believe we are not alone here on this earth. We all have many guides and angels around us from the non-physical world. It was now my time to open up to this relationship with my new found Spirit friend and teacher.

9

Sisterhood

My heart was calling for deeper love in all areas of my life. My illness had awakened me to this awareness. I was very challenged with the physical symptoms of a sick body but I disciplined myself to meditate and feel my emotional body each day. Louise Hay's book, *Heal Your Body*, provided me with great insight and direction for my recovery. I became more acutely aware of the power my thoughts had on my life and my body. As she explains in her book:

"Both the good in our lives and the dis-ease are the results of mental thought patterns which form our experience. We all have many thought patterns that produce good, positive experience and these we enjoy. It is the negative thought patterns that produce uncomfortable, unrewarding experiences with which we are concerned.

We have learned that for every effect in our lives, there is a thought pattern that precedes and maintains it. Our consistent thinking patterns create our experiences. Therefore, by changing our thinking patterns, we can change our experiences."[4]

I began using positive new thought patterns to heal the negative ones that manifested. These affirmations helped me bring more loving self-approval to myself, creating more ease. Slowly I began to feel better both physically and emotionally. I was alone with my children Luke and Lane a lot and felt maybe it was time to venture out and be more in the world.

The environment was still affecting me and I had to be cautious, yet I had prayed on this particular morning to connect with like-minded women. My body was feeling stronger and I thought that perhaps yoga or some sort of exercise class would help me in some way. I had always been active in aerobics and really missed it.

It was a glorious morning as I drove my daughter Lane to her first preschool class. The beauty of the sun shining on the water as I drove over the Manasota Key Bridge was breathtaking. I still have that feeling each time I make that trip. That morning I felt very open and so happy to be alive and living in my body. As I parked the car I noticed other women dressed in exercise clothing going into the building next door. Being curious, after I took Lane to her class, I peered through the window to find a room filled with women doing dancercise.

The teacher waved me in, introduced herself as Candy and invited me to join them. And so I did. When the class finished, another woman stood up and announced that her name was Liah and she was starting a women's meditation group in the area. Wow! I was very excited and now beginning to see the power of intent and prayer. Asking God or the Universe for what I wanted and letting go of the way it might show up seemed to be the key – because it often did show up! It was perfect timing for me because now I was ready for this new life. I had prayed for a teacher and Liah was not only that for me but she also became a friend. Our connection was beautiful and I felt safe to express my experiences with the non-physical world.

Her guidance sparked more life for me and her compassionate heart listened as she took me under her wing. Soon after I began her classes on meditation and psychic development, she invited me to join a women's circle. I know the group questioned having me there after learning how sensitive I was to chemicals. In order for me to be in the group, they would have to refrain from wearing perfumes and lighting candles. This experience was new for all of them and for me. Going out into the world gave me the opportunity to set boundaries for my own safety, while educating these women about my 20th century disease.

Meeting my "angel" sisters gave me the support I needed as I continued to embrace my truth. The loving purity of their hearts brought me the opportunities to share deep parts of myself without judgment. I had prayed for community, for women who understood where I was in my Spiritual journey and God brought me these amazing women.

Together we grew towards self-realization. It was a safe place for me to get in touch with my darkness and to get in touch with my gifts. Sometimes the experience was painful and some moments were pure bliss and others ranged everywhere in between. I was in the arms of the sisterhood and there I found comfort and some of that deeper love I had been searching for.

10

Do You Believe In Miracles?

Meditation had become a new and powerfully rich experience. Each day I would enter into that peaceful place within and ask questions with the hope of receiving guidance or insight from my guides or angels. And each time I would experience an energy much stronger than me begin to move through me. My pen would not stop as the voice inside me took over. It was as if I was taking dictation. Sometimes I would write a question at the top of a sheet of paper, and then the answer would simply flow onto the page below. When I stopped writing and began to read the words, it was as if someone was speaking directly to me.

I had become very comfortable with my communications with my guide Remos. But one day I felt the presence of another energy. I was enveloped by light, as unconditional love poured into my heart. I became lost in it while at the same time aware that this energy was Jesus. I felt the same, familiar love that has held me from the time I was a little girl praying to Jesus. I then saw Him standing before me in a luminous white robe. As Jesus spoke to me the light I was seeing in my third eye seemed to move right onto the page.

How I see with my third eye – my inner eyes – has always been with me. I imagine that it is much like a blind person would see. In the energy I receive information that appears in my mind. It is a sixth sense beyond what my physical eyes can experience but definitely not an illusion. I believe I have been able to see more in this way because I trust in the energy and acknowledge it.

I was an empty vessel for Jesus' love. The pen moved across the page without any connection to my conscious mind. I continued to write awash in the waves of magnificent love flowing through me. When I finally stopped writing, His words echoed inside my head and the energy filled my heart as Jesus told me that I would continue to write letters from Him.

It was not until later that I felt my resistance. I didn't want it to be Jesus because then the experience felt religious to me, instead of Spiritual. I was born and raised Catholic, yet I wanted to be far away from anything that was put in a box of organized religion. But the energy and the message were incredibly beautiful. I realized it wasn't Jesus I was resistant to, but rather the way I was taught religion through fear and guilt in Catholic school and at church.

I began to let go of my resistance and to open myself to the idea that Jesus would come to me. It was as if I did not feel quite worthy of the experience. But why not? I always spoke to Jesus and prayed to Jesus. Isn't He really talking to all of us through our hearts?

It became a routine. Each morning after I put my children on the school bus and did my meditation and yoga, I would sit down and open myself to receive a letter from Jesus. By now I was leading guided meditation groups and soon after I began my new morning routine, one of the women in my group told me she felt she was to help me by typing the letters I was receiving. Florence became an important support for me at this time. I would write page after page of messages from Jesus, and give them to Florence, who would send them back all typed in her computer and ready for a book one day. Florence was a student of *A Course In Miracles* and she told me the messages were very similar to *A Course In Miracles*, only in a simpler version.

A Course In Miracles (ACIM) was written by Helen Schucman, who heard a Voice and wrote what that Voice "said" to her. She would then read it to her friend Bill Thetford the next day at work. The whole process took seven years and this unedited piece of work has provided a way for some people to find their own teacher within. ACIM deals with universal Spiritual themes and principles and stresses that this is only one of the paths to God.

One day Florence phoned me in the middle of typing one of my letters. "Do you believe in miracles?" she asked. She then told me that while typing, she found a grammatical error. Since she felt hesitant to edit the words of Jesus, she went to her husband Darry for advice. He agreed that it was definitely an error. As she walked back to her computer carrying the letter she was transcribing, the words I had handwritten on the page changed. Right before her eyes, the error was corrected! It truly was a miracle!

These letters from Jesus helped me to begin trusting the voice of my inner teachers. So when I began to feel in my heart that I should start *A Course In Miracles* circle, I put the word out even though I wasn't a "real" instructor.

In a few weeks I had a weekly group. As the facilitator, I allowed The Voice to speak through me. At the end of the session I would open up *ACIM* and the text would always affirm everything that was shared that day. The purpose of *ACIM* is explained, step-by-step, at both the theoretical and practical levels. It emphasizes application rather than theory and experience rather than theology. It specifically states that, *"a universal experience is not only possible but necessary."*[5] This weekly group and the lessons from *ACIM* inspired me in every part of my life as it affirmed all of the truths I was receiving from my own inner teacher.

11

I Am the Book

Meditation helped me through the challenges that had brought me to Florida. I was committed every day to being quiet and touching parts of me that were longing to be felt. Before I opened my eyes I would breathe into my dream so I could ground it there in my memory. I was told that before one gets out of bed in the morning not to move, just be with the dream so it can show you its message.

I loved remembering the experience of the night. It felt like I was watching a movie. Then I would get up and sit at my altar in the corner of the bedroom, begin my prayer and open myself to meditation. This area was a sacred place for me and my altar was adorned with pictures and crystals. Around me, I wrapped the shawl that my grandmother crocheted for me when she was in her nineties, as I used my breath to take me deeper.

This morning time meditation brought so much understanding as I searched inside for answers. Visions and colors of light moved through my consciousness and I would leave then, to go on a spiritual journey beyond this world. I loved being in this state because I did not feel sick. I expanded through it and beyond it. I would pick up my journal when I felt vast and empty of thought and in the place of nothingness the words moved through me. I let my hand write. Time had no meaning here. I asked questions and the answers came without effort.

One morning I woke up very early and quietly slipped out of bed to go and meditate. Something was calling me and as I sat in stillness the light in my mind's eye got brighter and brighter. All of a sudden it seemed as if I were walking through a doorway into even brighter light. The love inside of me intensified and suddenly

I was surrounded by beings of light. A voice spoke to me saying, "Welcome home."

The love I was feeling was so powerful and it filled every part of me. I felt so in love as I heard myself say, "Can I stay here? I don't want to go back there." I couldn't believe that I had no interest in returning back to the life I was living. I wanted to stay in this place called 'home.' Then I heard them say to me, "No, you have to return to write a book which will bring humanity to this love you are feeling now!"

I thought, "I am not a writer, how can I write a book?" The next moment I was out of that sacred space and back in my bedroom. I cried because the encounter was so awesome. Yet I couldn't believe I was so willing to let go of my earthly life for what I had just experienced. I cried because I did not feel that love inside of me.

After that experience I was committed to writing every day. I thought everything I wrote was going to be in my book. Every word I wrote in my journals would touch the world in some way. I just kept showing up to write and the writing was teaching me. The energy and truth were healing me. It was expressing parts of me I hadn't developed or noticed. Every feeling, every experience showed me more truth about myself and about God. I was apprenticing with God as I learned how to express myself through this wonderful gift of the written word. I had always been an artist, yet now I was creating in an art form other then drawing or painting.

One day someone had phoned to book me to do a seminar. I got off the phone feeling insecure about my credentials. I felt if I only had a published book it could be easier to prove that what I do is worthwhile. It was in that moment I heard a voice inside saying, "*You are the book.*"

12

Our Issues Are In Our Tissues

Our history can feed us or it can destroy us. Our past traumas and fearful experiences, when not embraced or looked at, can create negative experiences in our current life. Yet when we are aware of our fears or those so-called negative experiences, we can change our minds about them. We can see the gift in the experience. When we embrace our past, we don't have to be afraid of the outside world, which is filled with wounded human beings just like ourselves. The wound, when touched and held sacred in our own loving hearts, can bring us to our conscious will. When we gain wisdom from our life experience and allow this wisdom to be our guide, we can then choose a different response, make a different choice, as we take care of ourselves in the world. We can be close with who we are and know that in the moment we are taking care of ourselves in a healthy way. Our fears can teach us a lot about ourselves. When we understand what created these fears – usually from our childhood – and what is triggering them in the present, we can take care of the inner child and the grown-up at the same time.

At this time on my healing journey, I was beginning to open up to the inner fears that were running my life. The laws of the universe are very powerful and the law of magnetic attraction in our life is seen all the time. Like attracts like. It is so interesting when I witness people who come to my meditation circles. While I am expressing what I am going through at that time and what I am embracing in my own personal life, most of the people who show up that night are going through a similar experience, or they have just come out of it. When I am feeling my fears, they seem to manifest in many areas of my life. Or life brings me the opportunity to feel what I am unconsciously vibrating within me.

These memories and mistaken beliefs about ourselves are held and locked in the body. We shoved these fear-based thoughts and experiences down into our bodies, when we were not ready to deal with them. It was too painful to feel. Often we didn't know how, or didn't have permission to feel these emotions as children. If the experiences were too traumatic, we left ourselves and left our own power. This is when we began to give our power away to something or someone outside of us.

This is what happened to me when I was young and I continued this pattern into my adult life when I was in fear. When I believed someone or something outside me had control, or I felt someone was projecting his or her own anger or fear onto me, I would leave emotionally. I often left my own heart and believed that something was wrong with me.

My body was sick and in pain, but now the emotions inside were calling for my attention. Finally, I began reaching out for help. Once my physical body began to get stronger and healthier, it was time to begin focusing on healing my emotional body. All of the powerful healing energy I was moving through me during my meditation experiences was bringing more unresolved issues to the surface. I began to receive bodywork, like massage and cranial sacral therapy, which is when some of my submerged memories started to become clearer. I began to understand some of the nightmares I had had since I was a little girl; the reoccurring dreams that brought certain fearful memories to me that I was terrified to embrace.

I can write about this part of my life now. I was sexually abused – once by a distant relative when I was a little girl and date raped twice in my teens and twenties. Going into the details of it isn't important anymore. There is a question, though, that lives within me: Why is this kind of abuse so common for women to experience throughout our life?

I was in my late thirties when I finally began uncovering this wound with the help of wonderful counselors, Jim DeMaio, Liah and Tim Howard. Awareness of these long-buried memories was important. I needed to touch the emotions and feelings that had been smoldering deep inside me for most of my life, taking away my power and making me sick.

These events were so traumatic for me as a young girl that I probably left my body so I wouldn't feel the hurt. But the feelings of fear, shame, anger and powerlessness were still there, nonetheless, suppressed and buried deep inside my body.

I think it is interesting that I began wearing glasses at the age of seven, which is when I was first sexually abused. I believe I didn't want to see or relive the experience, so my eyesight became affected. Like the fairy tale about *The Princess And The Pea*, the memory of this experience had now become a pea I could no longer ignore. But until my body became sick and toxic, I had very little memory of these experiences.

My relationship with Bob became more challenging and uncomfortable. I was uncomfortable with these new realizations and my emotions were overwhelming me as my anxieties and fears shut me down to him. I was afraid – and I had no understanding of why. It felt like I was making it all up. The more I would meditate and go inside, the more my life seemed uncomfortable. I began to use different modalities to release this feeling of discomfort and get back to peace. Working with my chakras (a Sanskrit word, meaning "wheel") helped me to understand and activate my body's seven main energy centers. Even though the body has hundreds of locations of focused and concentrated energy, these are the major ones.

Shirley MacLaine has a wonderful video about the chakras and the importance of energy flow through these spinning vortexes.

The chakras are the network through which our body, mind and Spirit interact as one holistic system. Each chakra corresponds and relates to one of the various glands of the body's endocrine system, as well as relating to one of the seven colors of the rainbow. These centers can become doorways through which our emotional, mental and Spiritual energies flow into the physical expression of our life. They are openings through which our attitudes and belief systems create our mind/body form. The energies, which are created from our own emotions and mental attitudes, run through the chakras and are then distributed into the cells, tissues and organs. Visualizing these chakra colors can help bring balance from the base of the spine to the head.

Whenever I felt my energy was blocked, I would put my attention on these areas. I'd lay my hands on my heart or any other center of my body and focus on the colors. This practice helped me to get back to the love. When we are in a state of unconditional love, these centers in our body are activated and begin to align.

I wanted and knew I needed help to embrace my deepest and darkest fears. I began seeing Jim De Maio for counseling and this is when I started doing more intense work with my inner child. Working with Jim was a safe place for me to let out these thoughts and feelings as I began to understand my fears. Jim was also very involved with A *Course In Miracles*, which made a good, harmonious match.

I loved how Jim would call me on the truth. He helped me see the illusions I was stuck in. I was often listening to my fear and my ego. Instead, I learned I could move myself into better perceptions that would support and guide me.

With Jim's help, I was able to see how, at a very young age, I learned to give my power away. In my fear, I would leave my body and go to my mind. He recommended a book by Charles Whitfield, entitled *Healing The Child Within*. It brought me greater insight, while helping me to embrace my past hurt and pain. I learned that in the past, I decided that something was wrong with me and I needed to be fixed. From that point on, the vibration of this self-judgment attracted experiences that resonated with this place of shame.

In truth, I was innocent, yet now I could take responsibility for the choices I had made. In Gary Zukav's book, *Seat Of The Soul*, he points out that when we make a conscious choice, we are responsible for ourselves and the consequences that go along with our choices. [6]

That idea really resonated with me. Now that I was touching these feelings of my inner child, I could grow up and make choices to support the grown-up me. It is amazing how we go into a kind of insanity and completely forget who we are when we are in our fears. By touching the blocked memories and fears, I came to know there was nothing wrong with me. In releasing myself from that place of shame, I was giving myself unconditional love; I was no longer judging myself. And where there is love, there is no room for fear because the two emotions cannot co-exist in the same space.

Feeling myself without conditions was a powerful place to be. I was beginning to feel freedom in my body. There was more space for my creative force to flow through in the moment. Self-love is telling myself that I am okay just as I am. As author Dr. Michael Ryce says –A sin is a mistaken belief about yourself that you are separate from love. God made you so powerful that you will create an experience to bring up this mistaken belief about yourself so that you can return to the truth. The truth being that God never left you. You left your own heart – your own true power of love.[7]

The feeling that I was abandoned or abused brought me back to myself. I continued to create relationships that brought these feelings to me and slowly I realized I did not have to be a victim any longer. I could make choices to support me and to take care of me. When I forgot my center, my own love, I would allow myself to be the object of someone else's hurt and pain. I would take it personally. My healing showed me how to stay centered. Then I would remember that another person's fears and anger are all their own – and really have nothing to do with me. If I feel uncomfortable, that is my reaction. It is my responsibility to own my feelings, take care of myself and choose a different reaction the best way I can.

My life had been one long continuous experience created by a victim – me. Opening myself up to be present with what was true in the moment connected me to the creative force inside. Just because we may have been abused doesn't mean we have to abuse. This seems to be a pattern for victims. We can heal our own wounds so that there isn't a place inside us that another abuser can plug into. I could tap into this truth all the time and feel connected to the universal life force. When you heal, others have an opportunity to heal too!

So began my healing of myself as a sexual being and not a needy little girl trying to fill a void – a dark hole of pain and hurt and loneliness. I learned as a very young girl to shove my feelings deep inside, covering up my fear of living in this big world filled with other wounded adult children. I only felt safe to feel my sensuality on the outside and being a fashion model fed me in some external way. But I didn't feel it from the inside until I began to touch this dark place. I was a model, but inside I did not feel my beauty at all.

My own life's physical and emotional pain brought me the key that helped free me from my self-imposed prison. Awareness was the key that opened me to the truth. Each of us is totally in charge of the way we perceive and see things by the words we use to describe or interpret the events in our life. Our minds can touch many levels at the same time. The trick is to bring it all into consciousness, change our reaction and retrain our thinking.

It sure didn't happen overnight, but step-by-step I was healing the layers and beginning to change my mind and perceptions about my life. It was time that I got in touch with my internal power. Each of us is responsible for creating our own reality – maybe not the event, but how we experience and respond to that event.

They say God only gives us what we can handle and maybe our own process is the same way. We go deeper to find the truth when we are ready to live it.

When I first remembered these events and feelings, Jim De Maio told me I would continue to shut down to another's anger until I embraced my own. Up until this time, I was terrified of another's anger because I feared my own anger inside me. I would rather cry than feel the emotion of anger. The fear would paralyze me and I would become totally weak and helpless.

I remember being on the floor with pillows trying to perform an anger release process. I was encouraged to pound my anger and rage into the pillows, but I couldn't. I just crumbled into my tears and felt no strength in my body. Suppressed anger can cause all kinds of disease in the body. In Jim's book, *Helping Not Fixing*, he writes about anger:

"Maybe we need to stop doing something or begin to do something. We procrastinate when we are too afraid to make the change. This produces a loss of our peace and we begin to experience anger. We lose our peace to make the change but we are listening to the fearful self instead ... So anger is our best friend since it makes clear when we have an opportunity for growth not only in trusting our true self but increasing the quality of our life. It takes some courage to deal with our anger. Sometimes it's difficult just facing it and admitting it to others, not to mention the change involved.

"(Rage:) Anger that has been repressed or hidden from our awareness will take on a character for itself and be acted out in an uncontrolled fashion. This is often embarrassing because we are not aware of what we are doing. Most people confuse rage and anger. This is why they refuse to deal with their anger. They are afraid of rage. Rage is a clear call for help. Unfortunately, most others are frightened away before they see the rageful person's need."[8]

It is amazing to me to think that a single moment in time can affect us for the rest of our lives when we stay victims of the event. Taking responsibility for me means simply knowing I was young and it happened. What could I do about it now? Feel the emotions – the sadness, the anger. Feel, feel, feel. Accept that it is a part of my life. No, what happened to me was not right, but I was too young to defend myself.

This reminds me of a period of time when my son Luke was seven years old. He was projecting a lot of anger at his sister and me and then when he joined a summer theater camp, everything intensified. One morning he burst into tears, slamming things in his bedroom. He said, "Mommy, I can't go to camp because I get all these feelings when I look at the teacher."

His teacher was young with a revealing cleavage and I immediately realized the feelings he spoke of were sexual. He was crying and afraid. What was he trying to tell me? I did not understand. He said he saw all these pictures in his mind. I asked him, "What pictures? Please explain."

He began to tell me what he saw and then he screamed, "God, get these pictures out of my mind!"

It seemed to me he was seeing sexual, pornographic pictures that were way too advanced for such a young boy. I could feel the fear coming into me. Had he been abused in some way, like me? Or was this coming through from another life? After we shared more, I could see that he really was this innocent child who was angry at something he just did not understand.

For weeks Luke could not go to sleep unless we meditated and I held him in bed. He wanted to stop the pictures that would flash into his mind. His father spoke to him with compassion and I prayed for answers. Night after night we would have these horrific evenings with Luke crying and being angry at God, begging us to help him find peace.

One night after he finally got to sleep, I went into my bedroom, lit a candle and prayed for guidance and healing. That night was a different experience because in my visions I saw Jesus holding Luke in the water as if he was being baptized or cleansed. Then, peace filled my whole body. The silence of the night was broken when Luke came screaming and running into my room. Slamming the door open, Luke cried, "Mommy! Mommy! Jesus said everything was going to be alright!" Then he just melted into my arms. Later, Bob and I took him back to his own bed.

The next morning he got up saying he remembered where he saw the pornographic pictures. There was an older boy that had lived across the street from us in Canada. One day, when his grandmother was asleep, he had showed Luke his father's pornographic videos. The mystery was solved and there was healing for Luke.

We don't always have control over things that happen, but if we can let go of the hurt, the experience can help strengthen us in our life, rather than cripple us. My own healing had helped me unblock so I did not shut down when faced with Luke's anger and fears around his sexuality. I was able to help him touch his pain – because I had finally touched my own.

13

Healthy Self-Esteem

The greatest gift we can give to ourselves and to those around us is good health; to be healthy at all levels – body, mind and Spirit. Achieving this kind of health is seldom easy.

As I approach the age of fifty, I am finally comfortable being a sexual and sensual woman. I have not always believed it and have not always felt safe with it. Sexuality has always been a confusing subject for me. I was not healthy in that area. I was wounded.

Through the process of my deep emotional, physical and Spiritual work, I have come to understand the role that sexuality has played in my life. From my searching and self-discovery, I have received truth from many different teachers, guides and Spirit. To begin healing the wounds around my sexuality, I had to deal with the emotional and physical trauma left behind from the sexual abuse in my childhood. At the age of fifteen, my parents enrolled me in a self-improvement course because they wanted to do something to help me develop stronger self-esteem. When I look back on those years, I can see clearly I was not very present with myself. My sexuality was projected out into the world to get validation. I realize now I was a wounded little girl who looked for Divine Love outside of myself, instead of connecting with this powerful energy inside to heal and create a strong aura around me.

The Dark Side Of The Light Chasers, by Debbie Ford, is a wonderful book that has taught me a lot. In it she writes beautifully on the topic of the shadow self – the parts of our selves that we hide and have trouble owning. My life brought to me people that flirted and projected their sexuality to get attention. As I did this healing work, I saw in these people a quality that I had. I also saw how I judged this quality in them and I how I had not embraced it in myself. When I saw it manifested in another person, it was easier for me to blame them. Now I am able to see the gift they were for me. As I meditated on this new awareness, I could see the times I had unconsciously dishonored other relationships because of my own needy little girl who was just striving to get love. The shadow in me was the sexually wounded child who did not own her own sexual energy. Even though I was not aware of her or of this energy, I projected it out into the world. Unconsciously, I was after a quick fix, something to fill that very deep hole of pain and hurt. If I couldn't feel it within myself, I would plug into another wounded soul that I hoped would give me the love I was searching for.

It is not easy to write these truths, but I own them now.   I realize I am all of my brothers and sisters who have not fully owned the power of energy that is within. A big part of healing my physical body has been to own my sexual energy - the kundalini, the life force (the yogic term for 'primary life force'). Swami Sivananda Radha defines it this way: *"Kundalini means 'that which is coiled up.' This is an energy that is lying dormant at the base of the spine."*[9] It is also called the prana (a Sanskrit word for 'life air' or 'life force'). This is such powerful energy and if we do not believe in ourselves and our own connection to Divine Spirit, then there will be a wound, a place within us for other wounded individuals to plug into. It is our birthright to have a healthy relationship with our sexual energy. This energy, when felt in our root or base chakra, can be moved into our bellies to balance the male and female energies within, our ch'i.

In her book, *Sacred Contracts*, Caroline Myss describes ch'i as *"the vital energy that is circulated through and stored within the body and the breath itself. This vital energy is often viewed as an impersonal force emanating from the magnetic energy source of the universe. The Easterners believe they can facilitate the flow of prana (literally "breath of life") and ch'i through meditation and physical exercise, including breath control."*[10]

When we move energy, our own force field expands, touching our third chakra and embracing our fears, all the mistaken beliefs we have of our own connection to source - Divine Spirit. When our fears are touched by this energy, it opens our heart center, allowing our higher and lower chakras to unite. We are here to be grounded in this energy; to let love in, which creates a space for healing. This energy is our healer and when we own it for ourselves we can share it with others in a very healthy way.

I embraced my anger. I had anger at the man who violated me when I was a young girl; I had anger at the men that had allowed their sexual energy to be more powerful than my own physical strength as a women. I had anger at myself for allowing people to treat me without respect. I had anger at myself for forgetting who I am. And, I know deep in my heart that feeling this anger, allowing it to come up and out and releasing it from my body, helped me to heal myself and so change my life in such a healthy way.

I no longer choose to project my anger or my sexual energy out onto others. I own them; they are both a part of me that I am here to embrace. I have no need or desire to beat myself up anymore for my own lack of self-love. I love myself in these places and when I do, I can embrace the darkness too! I now choose to live my life as it was meant to be lived. One of God's greatest gifts to us is the power of choice. Healing can help you grow up and make good choices based on wisdom and knowledge, with faith and the energy of your Spirit.

Before my illness, I was unaware that my lack of self-love had made my life about getting validation from outside myself. My journey of healing has brought me to the wisdom that healthy self-esteem, self-love, is about loving *all* of myself, not just including, but *especially* the dark places. In this new place of self-acceptance and self-validation, the power of my Spiritual/sexual energy now opens my heart to inspire others to be all that they are and all that they can be.

14

Who Cares Who Brings the Message, As Long As I Listen?

Amazingly, my new friend, Liah helped me understand the communication I was receiving from the other side. This circle of women became the safe place to let the voice come through me. I began to realize that I was a medium for the non-physical world as I received messages for other people, as well as for myself. The fear and uncertainty sometimes made it difficult for me to share what I heard and saw. As I went beyond this fear and shared what I received, I got confirmation as these truths helped others. My greatest challenge was to trust and not worry about whether I would be judged or not. Because I was afraid I would not be accepted, I was cautious and less confident. But the more I surrendered and let go of the outcome, the more the experience healed others and me.

On Sanibel Island, off the southwest coast of Florida, there was a retreat called The Center for Transformation. I loved to go there because it was a safe place for me to share my new-found gift. The owners, Ann and Arthur Cataldo, became wonderful teachers for me. The women I met on these retreats inspired me, as I became more comfortable with this new path to spiritual truth. My children were young at the time and it was good to get away to this soul-nurturing place. These days, I often think of Ann who has since passed away. She was one of my mentors.

Ann channeled an entity named Simon and traveled the world to share the energy and wisdom of this remarkable guide. I loved going to her retreat and her home, because there, I was able to find more of me. When I asked Simon questions, I received so much insight. Ann was doing what I had just begun doing, yet she was very comfortable with her gift. As a novice, I had yet to fully understand it. As Ann shared with her groups all the energy and love that came through, I was being shown the way.

On my first retreat, Liah accompanied me. I woke up early one morning and was inspired to draw. I had brought colored felt pens with me and I began to draw purple angels. The angels looked different from any I had ever drawn in the past and I simply let it flow through.

Later that morning, the women gathered for meditation. As we sat in our circle, hands joined, everyone chanted the ancient mantra 'Om.' I felt myself slip into a slightly altered state. My hands felt as big as the Universe and soon the sounds moved me into the light. The light was purple and it got brighter and brighter as I began to see a vision of a woman clearly in my mind's eye. She said to me over and over again, "You don't have to die from this body to be the light."

The energy got very strong and it seemed Liah somehow knew what was happening. She asked the group to stop chanting so I could bring through the message. In the silence that followed, I began to speak. In this altered state, I said this woman's name was Susan. I described what she looked like and shared the words she wanted me to communicate. The woman holding my hand to my right suddenly burst out crying. Through her tears she told us this woman was a dear friend who had just died and her funeral was to be at noon that day. She told us Susan was an artist who had owned an art gallery. One day she decided to sell everything, wrote a will and took off to live her lifelong dream of going to India. Soon after she arrived in India, she got pneumonia and died. The woman told me Susan's artwork was famous – for her purple angels.

I was so excited, I went to my room and brought back the drawings I had done that morning. I had questioned this new style of drawing, but now I saw the bigger picture. This confirmation helped me to let go and trust. As my friend Liah had once said to me, this information is not just for me. I am here to share it with the world.

15

In the Present, I Am the Presence

Why do I not remember a lot of my childhood? I have asked myself this question many times because when my identical sister Colleen would share an incident from her childhood, I would be shocked to discover it had happened to her - and not to me. I had thought it was my memory, but when I would discover these incidents and memories were not mine, but hers, I would be shattered. Where was I? What was I doing as my life passed by? "The Snake Story" is an incident typical of what I am talking about.

All of my younger years I believed this experience happened to me, but Colleen swears it happened to her. Our Dad said he knew who it was, but would only reveal it in his will. We were even on a talk show where they spotlighted multiple births and as they interviewed my dad, he said he would not give the answer on national television. (Actually, I don't think he really knows, because it was so difficult to tell us apart, especially when we were young.)

The story goes like this:

We were up at our aunt and uncle's cottage one summer and there was a convenience store where they sold lots of penny candy. Being a child and going in with ten cents was great fun. On that day, I left with ten cents worth of black balls in a brown paper bag. I felt so happy sucking on these hard black candies that were licorice tasting at the beginning and then later turned into different colored layers of sugar. Yum!!!! I was happy as a lark walking down the dirt road back to the cottage when all of a sudden there was a snake in front of me on the side of the road. To my childish eyes it seemed twelve feet long and I was terrified. I began running and that snake was right behind me, chasing me. It followed me right to the cottage! I remember seeing the porch and the screen door and screaming for help. My dad came out as I raced inside to safety. He quickly got a shovel and killed the snake.

Now I remember every moment of this experience and I am sure it happened to me. I can still taste those black balls! But Colleen tells the same story and she believes it happened to her. Am I so connected to Colleen that I experienced the whole thing through her? Was I not present in my own life? Or was I so present that I felt everything in this presence? These are questions that I continue to ponder. As the years pass, I feel I understand myself more clearly, but I continue searching for the answers to understand more of this mystery. Maybe the truth is, I actually don't need to know.

We are all able to tap into the vastness of energy that some call God, the Universe, all that is, or essence. We are one speck of physical or human being in this vast energy of infinite possibility. When I became ill and my body was so full of physical symptoms, I found meditation. It enabled me to leave my physical and emotional bodies for the light, that pure essence, where I felt the vastness of God's presence. It was wonderful to leave all those dense feelings and physical symptoms behind. In that place of light, I would hear and see messages that guided and helped me understand what was going on inside me and in my life. I loved being out there. I was not grounded at all. I would leave my body and not come back for hours.

I remember an evening with my sisters when I was guiding them in a meditation. I went to that place I loved, that place far beyond this physical world. My sisters tried to bring me back and I could hear them, but it felt so great I wanted them to just let me be there. All of a sudden I was shocked back into my body as Philomene poured cold water on me. She was afraid I would leave and never come back, just like when I had chemical poisonings. I would get into that catatonic state and there was little connection back to this body and the world I was part of.

Out of my body, I felt relief from my sickness and the stresses of my life. I would be far beyond the pain of my body and my marriage. In that vast realm of love and comfort, I would receive guidance, insight and understanding. Great wisdom would pour through to me and I would write for hours. Yet later when I read the words, it seemed as if something or someone outside of me had written it.

I loved it. I loved the experience of asking a question and receiving words of wisdom that helped me understand this mystery of God, the presence and all that is. I was the messenger. I brought messages to many that asked for help. Yet my body was still sick. I was not getting better. I still had extreme episodes of physical illness that sometimes paralyzed me. This strong beautiful energy that I spiraled into would lift me up and then drop me into deeper despair the next day. I did not understand why. Touching all this vast energy was so blissful, so full of love. Yet when I came back into my body and my life, all the pain was still there.

So meditation became a drug too! I talked to a friend who told me the state of exhaustion that he loved to get into was also a drug – an addiction. An addiction can be anything that numbs us from feeling what is really going on – religion, endless therapy, running, watching television, eating and shopping... as well as the common ones like drugs, smoking, sex and alcohol. These addictions can keep you numb to what is really going on inside yourself and in your life.

My sister Philomene was the grounded one. She knew that I was not grounding this energy into me. How could I? I did not have enough space to allow it to enter. I wasn't staying present enough. I always believed that my heart was my grounding cord. We are here to be in our heart and breathe into our root and our belly and feel our life force, our sexual energy. To feel that red energy, the passion to be in the body. To live fully present in the now is to bring all of the vastness here. In order to do this I had to feel these painful feelings that were created from the mistaken beliefs that I was not this energy of God, of essence, of pure love. And as long as I was out of my body, I was still avoiding feeling all that pain.

Slowly, I began to feel my own self worth. I began to open myself to feel the red energy of anger and yes rage. As I began to feel all of the hurt and pain of my life, it overwhelmed me and I screamed and cried with greater intention, to get it out of my body. I embraced the feelings without judgment so that love could enter the empty space they left behind. When I felt sick or I had a chemical poisoning I would become emotional and feel all my fears. Learning to let these fears have a voice began my connection with my inner child.

Now I understood. When we shove our feelings down into our body and don't feel, we get sick and vulnerable. This sickness breaks us down and forces us to begin to feel. My sickness had opened me to feeling my self-hatred and the anger of not receiving the love I wanted as a child. And then, I held the child in her pain and stopped abandoning her by leaving my body. I held my child as I felt the truth – that little Frannie was a precious child of God. Like every child, she holds the key to the kingdom of heaven. To stay in my body, feel my emotional pain and let it all come out in a safe place enabled me to breathe into more of me. All of the control of keeping these terrible feelings suppressed had drained my life force. But slowly I began to touch these dark parts of me and in that place of unconditional love; I freed myself to see the truth. All of those people that I had perceived as not loving me and hurting and projecting pain on me were not *able* to love me. Just like me, they could not love themselves, so how could they possibly love me?

As I touched these painful places, I created more space for me to be present with this vast presence I was a part of. As I embodied this wonderful spiritual energy I felt healed. This Energy of Spirit can be rooted and grounded in the present moment through our heart and in this physical body. Our conscious breath can be our connection back to self.

16

Take Me Home

I went to a concert at Ticia's home, where all of my angel sisters were gathered. A singer songwriter named Matisha, who traveled internationally sharing his love through gifts of music and song, was going to perform. When I arrived that night, I knew I needed some healing. I found a place away in a corner where I could be with myself and the music. My eyes were closed when he began to sing. Soon, my heart expanded with the sound and I began to weep. His words reflected the depth of my soul. He sang like an angel and the energy moved through every cell of my body. I felt a deep connection with my heart and as my eyes opened, I looked right into Matisha's eyes. I knew him inside of me and it was a reunion of love, a part of me.

Soul family seems to meet this way. It is a recognition. This experience brought me to a part of myself that had been dormant for a long time. Matisha was singing a song he wrote called, *I See Your Beauty* and the vibration opened me as he sang, *You Are the Love You are Seeking*. Each song opened me more to the language of my heart. The lyrics to *The Eyes of Home* brought me deeper into myself, as I felt the energy of the dolphins. Feeling free in my self and in my heart, I felt happier than I had felt for a long time.

It was exciting to be with all these people, singing the songs of my soul. We were all in one heart loving, as we sang the lyrics together. Joy welled up inside of me, as I brought my friend Chris Adams into my heart, knowing he was so sick and wanted to be here with me that night. He had AIDS and had entered the hospital the day before with pneumonia. As I sang, I held him in my mind, knowing he would have loved the evening's experience.

Matisha asked us all to sit with a partner and look into their eyes as we sang the words repeating, "When I look into your eyes you reflect the love for me."

"Joy's my name, love's my game!" my partner said. It was clear to me she was sent by God. She called me "child of my heart" and I felt our lifetime of connections; a mother's love, even though she is my friend and companion on earth now. Joy's unconditional love beamed straight to my heart. I saw through her eyes my children, my husband and my friend Chris who was in the hospital that night.

Tears washed through me. I was being birthed into my own true love. I touched the beloved in me as I looked into my beloved's eyes. I understood that night what self-love truly meant. This love has no judgment. It has no form, it is a reflection from within that we can see and feel with everyone. That night was something I had never experienced before. All of our energies weaving together, as this new friend Matisha facilitated music that came from each of our hearts. The ethereal music was bringing me into more love each moment. It was ecstasy and I felt so alive and inspired to live in this way, in all ways. I couldn't wait to share Matisha's music with Chris.

Meeting Matisha that night was an adventure. He shared his music with us in such a magical way. Very early the next morning I received a call from Chris' mom. Chris had died that night and she hoped I would speak for him at his funeral. Chris had told her I knew what he had learned from his dying. Through my tears I said I would, but I did not yet know what Chris meant.

A little later, the phone rang again and it was Matisha. He called immediately when he woke and said he had dreamt I was crying. His perception blew me away. He knew what I was feeling and we had only just met the evening before.

I cried more for the loss of my young friend who had just passed, while my new friend held the space for me, reminding me to breathe. He wanted to come and see me, but I said no. Someone was coming to view our house, which was for sale and I had a lot to do. "Thank you for what you brought me," I told him, as I said goodbye.

I called my neighbor and dear friend, Sandie, who had been at the concert with me and she came to help me clean. We put on Matisha's music and grieved for our friend Chris.

Sandie had introduced me to Chris one day at the Unity church. After the service, she hardly recognized Chris when he greeted her. They had worked at a restaurant in Venice, Florida together. He told us he had been very ill, but was recovering and had come to Unity to learn to meditate. I was standing beside Sandie, so she introduced me and said, "Here's your teacher. Frannie facilitates meditation circles in this area. She will teach you."

Chris and I spent time together doing one-on-one sessions. He shared his fear of dying of AIDS. He told me truths about himself he had never told anyone. He was embracing his demons, like Debbie had the night before she died, while lying in her mother's arms. And while Chris bared his soul, I held the space for him to connect with his own true nature of love.

Sandie and I were thinking about Chris as we listened to one of Matisha's songs called *Take Me Home*. I became so excited, I screamed with joy. I knew in that moment I had met Matisha to share his song with the people who would gather at the service. The words were so appropriate and would help those who loved Chris feel the part of him that he had allowed me to know.

That night, I sat in meditation asking God what I should say. Chris was a new friend and yet one that shared so much truth in his dying. He was such a beautiful, courageous man. He was only in his twenties and so alive, even near the end. He had so wanted to heal and live more fully in this life. He had wanted to forgive himself and his past.

This disease had given him his connection to what was real. I meditated, waiting for something in my silence. I began to see a dove in my inner vision and then I felt Chris' presence and his love poured through me. I heard him say to me telepathically,

"When you see the dove, I will speak through you." I felt very calm and totally at peace.

The next day I drove with Sandie and shared what I had received. This was all still new to me - sharing communications from other dimensions. I told Sandie I was nervous and that I didn't know what I would say. I just trusted and with her sitting beside me, I felt her love and support. The moment came when I was asked to go to the pulpit. I looked out over the crowd of people gathered and was very afraid. All of a sudden, as I stood before his family and friends, my vision blurred and I didn't see anyone. Out of the darkness I saw light, which became a beautiful white dove with its wings spread hovering over the congregation. My eyes just focused on this vision. As the energy moved into my heart, I began to speak. I knew this was Chris' energy that had entered me to communicate to all his loved ones.

All of the truths he learned in his dying freed his Spirit. He was home in the light of the One. I ended the message with Matisha's song, *Take Me Home*. Many were overwhelmed by love and tears and we were joined together in our hearts. That song brought Chris' message home to every heart that was present. Many of his family and friends ordered the tape so they could remember the beautiful messages Chris brought to all of us with his living. We all gathered in celebration of his life, not in mourning over his death. In our hearts, through Chris' heart, we return home in God's love.

Take Me Home

Here I stand on the edge of my life's glory
So much to see, even more
than I could ever say
All of us, every moment have before us,
the same choices
All of us, every day, call for love
with many voices

Take me Home I'm ready now
Take me Home Lord I'm ready now
It doesn't have to mean that my body dies
Take me Home I'm ready now
Take me Home Lord I'm ready now
Let it mean I join with love and my Spirit flies

All the reasons, now they're ending
for why I'd separate myself from you
All the seasons, what they're sending,
reflections of the truth that we all change
All of us every moment have before us the same choices
All of us, every day call for love with many voices

Take me Home I'm ready now
Take me Home Lord I'm ready now
It doesn't have to mean that my body dies
Take me Home I'm ready now
Take me Home Lord I'm ready now
Let it mean I join with love and my Spirit flies
All of us every moment have before us the same choices

From the album, "Love All The Way" by Matisha.
Website: http://SongofHome.com

17

Feeling My Beauty From the Inside

Matisha's friendship connected me with my Mt. Shasta family and eventually created the experience of swimming with my dolphin family in Hawaii. Life began to open for me in ways I had only dreamed of. I began to live more fully in my body and I was more conscious of the choices I made, allowing them to emerge from the highest truth, my soul-self, rather than my fear. What my heart guided me to do was take the risk and leap into the abyss of unknowing. This was frightening because I had to let go of what I thought was security. I had to trust my source.

The day I left to go to Sedona and then Mt. Shasta with my angel sisters, Ticia, Azura and Cheryl, was one of those leaps that changed my life. The women who attended my groups, my Circle of Angels, gave me the trip as a gift for my fortieth birthday.

The night before our departure, my friend Azura had a dream: all four of us were running towards the edge of a cliff, but only I jumped without hesitation, as the others watched me dive into the beyond. Wow! In retrospect, that is exactly how this trip felt to me. I knew I had to go forward, into what I did not yet know, but there was an energy moving me I could not deny.

On the day of our departure, energy and excitement coursed through me, as well as a little fear. Whatever lay ahead, I knew it would change my life. When we arrived at the airport, my spine tingled as we approached the departure gate. The sign at the gate read "11:11!" Over the years, "11:11" has come to be both a personal symbol and a major road sign from Spirit for me. The symbol represents a gateway into infinite possibilities. As author Solara explains in her book *11:11 Inside the Doorway*, "(11:11) is about completion, graduation, mastery, empowerment, embodying our Highest Truth, freedom, sacred union, True Love, One Heart,

Oneness...The 11:11 is the bridge to an entirely different spiral of energy patterning."[11]

Many times when a moment was meaningful or I was to pay attention, I noticed the clock read "11:11." On this day when I saw it, my heart began to beat wildly. I knew Spirit was telling me to take the risk, pay attention and trust my life to unfold as divinely planned.

I believe the purpose of my trip to Arizona was to help me let go of past attachments and ground the Goddess Energy through my own heart center, into the red rocks of Sedona. There I reclaimed my feminine energy and felt empowered in the energy of unconditional love.

Before we left Sedona, we had been informed of an Ascension workshop given by Ashtar Athena which we learned was almost over – only one day left. We told them we were from Florida and hoped to attend that last day. After speaking with us briefly, Athena gave her permission. When we arrived, we were surprised to see the large number of people from all over the U.S. and Canada. We sat with a hundred or more people, not knowing what to expect. Athena began to embody Ashtar fully and he spoke through her in the most powerful way. Her mannerisms became more masculine and very direct. She approached me immediately saying: "How dare you feel unworthy to channel the energy of our brother, Jesus?"

I was very startled and taken aback. No one knew I had been doing this – bringing messages from Jesus to my Angel Sisters and writing letters from Jesus daily in my journal.

Remembering my "11:11" symbol, I surrendered and opened my heart fully to Athena's vibration. She gently received the messages from Ashtar, who then in front of every one in the room, spoke through her directly to me. He told me it was time for me to begin what I was here to do – share the energy with all. I was to stop straddling the fence, one foot in God's energy, the other firmly attached to the material world and my own attachments to other people's opinions.

This major career change was nothing I had consciously planned; yet I was conscious even then that doing this work was a place where love danced more deeply in me. To embody the living vibration of unconditional love for others and myself was my joy. And now I was being told it was time to do it - openly and freely - for all who came to me.

The next day I consciously allowed more of the energy to move through me. Every moment I felt and saw more energy in my waking state. As I was now more grounded in my body, I was able to bring through more of my higher vibration into this physical dimension. My soul was living consciously and I was healed in Spirit's presence. I was eating, walking, talking, yes dancing the new freedom that love of self had given me. I was high on love's energy and I was ready to share it.

The next part of our journey was to a retreat at Mt. Shasta. There we joined new friends waiting to meet us. Going to Mt. Shasta was a safe place to begin to live as my true self. What a Divine setup it turned out to be!

As we joined the group at the retreat, it felt like coming home to me. My heart was wide open and I was excited and nervous at the same time. Quietly and inwardly I heard Jesus whisper words directly to my heart, telling us we should enter the retreat like deer, gently merging our energy with theirs. It felt like we were all in one consciousness, one energy, sharing the same inner and outer experiences. It was all so freeing! It was like slipping into garments of love and walking in heaven with all these new friends - our new family. The gifts were enormous and each meeting was a re-minding and remembering of my heart self, which longed to love in a deeper way. I was so grateful to meet the beautiful souls who would continue to nurture me later, when I forgot the truth.

My Goddess Energy was healing my body and I truly felt my beauty from the inside. Everyone and everything I saw was a beautiful reflection of God. As a group of many, we traveled in silence along the path to Panther Meadow at the foot of Mt. Shasta. A beautiful Garden of Eden, it was a place of sacred communion, where earth danced with heaven. This land is so sacred – the waterfalls birthing streams; wildflowers shining their faces to the sun, all guiding us to walk in honor of the earth.

Ticia, Azura, Cheryl and I found a huge boulder to rest upon. With the sun gently touching our skin, it was pure bliss. Ticia was the first to take off her clothing and I immediately followed. It seemed like the most natural thing in the world as we allowed our nakedness to join with nature all around us. It felt so free!

Ticia, who was so comfortable with her own body, was my teacher bringing me to more of myself. I could hear the music of flutes, guitars and harps weaving through my heart – all the sounds of my heart in love with God and of God loving me. Remaining in silence, we broke bread together and joined with others, being so present with self.

As a mother with two children, dinnertime at my home was anything but silent. But in this place, it felt wonderful to have time to just be with myself. I felt no shyness about my body and I felt my womanhood feeding me. People are always surprised to learn that all my life I had never felt pretty enough. I thought my body was too skinny and had always been very self-conscious. As a professional model, my body was constantly compared to others and judged. But here in this sacred place, for the very first time, I truly felt myself from the inside. I did not care what I looked like. I felt a part of everyone and everything. It felt perfect to be naked and free and my heart sang its joy in celebration of being with these people. It was like being in the Garden of Eden with nothing to hide because the energy of our true essence was all the clothing we needed.

Everyone gathered after dinner under a huge tent at a place called Stewart Mineral Springs. It was a cool night. There were approximately seventy people sitting on chairs in a large circle, as the evening session was a sharing of gifts and talents. Some danced and sang, or presented their poetry, all expressions of their love. I decided to just enjoy everyone who participated in the sharing, to simply be witness to the event. I really didn't want to do anything but receive.

After about an hour of watching different participants, there came a silent space where no one got up to share. All of a sudden I felt hands pushing me into the center of the circle. It felt as if time stood still. What was going on?

I saw a beam of light coming down from the ceiling of the tent we were in. I reached my hand up, touched the light, and then placed my hand on my heart. Walking towards the group, I began speaking the words that were flowing through me.

"I am the light of Christ, you are the light of Christ, we are the love of Christ." As I moved in front of each person, I looked into their eyes and each gaze opened me to an even greater flow of love. The energy was already incredible, but it continued to build. This enormous flow of love poured through me into each person; I could see the light shining in every person I passed. The words I spoke came from somewhere deep in the inner silence within me, touching the heart of each soul present. Everyone held the space for me to do what I was being guided to do. I felt connected to everyone; I felt I knew them without knowing them. I was beautifully present with myself and with each person, more than I had ever experienced in this body before.

When I finished going around the circle I returned to my chair and sat down. For a few moments, I was aware of feeling embarrassed. What had just happened? Yet the love was still so deep and overpowering.

When the evening came to a close, a man approached me and acknowledged my experience. "You showed me an empowered woman," he said. "Don't forget who you are." His name was Gary Zukav. I did not yet know him from his books or his Spiritual teachings; I felt I had just met one of my soul family. It was an instant love I felt with him. I had just experienced the embodiment of more of my essence and the sharing of this love with each person had further healed me. Later I learned Gary was one of the facilitators of the event.

The retreat presented one gift after another. The last night I needed a place to sleep before departing for home. Gary offered his living room. There was a beautiful painting of Jesus on the wall in the living room. As I looked at it, light seemed to emanate from it. This picture drew me in by its light and energy.

Before going to sleep I meditated, wondering about life and its adventures. Later, from a deep sleep, I awakened in the light. It seemed as if the walls of Gary's house were gone and there was just light everywhere. I heard a voice from deep within, a familiar voice saying, "You are activated in the Christ light; go and share this love with all creation." The light got brighter, a flame burning inside me; I felt as if every cell of my body was in communication with Spirit. I was hearing my past, my present and my future all at once. In that one eternal moment, I understood it all.

The love was so beautiful, I stayed awake for the rest of the night. The golden light was so present it brought me to tears. I wept freely, as this deep love continued to flow.

When Gary got up and came into the living room that morning, I will never forget his words, "You are radiating golden light," he said. He saw what I was feeling. When I shared my experience with him, he said, "Now you will share this with the world."

But how would I do that?

That morning we went to Morningstar, where Shalomar and Grace lived in the meadow at the foothills of Mt. Shasta, a little piece of heaven. Shalomar is a songwriter and a musician and Grace a poet and healer. Gary said he saw the light coming from me; I felt as if I was walking in the fourth dimension. Then, I shared my experience with my new friends.

Here on the sacred mountain, I felt so comfortable. Many call Mt. Shasta "the guru." If you've got stuff, the mountain will be the energy to show it to you. It is such a powerful place to be. But it was time for me to leave this place where I felt safe to embody more of my true self. Now I was going to begin to live this love. Just how I would do that, I did not yet know. I was afraid and excited all at the same time, yet there was a knowingness in me that gave me the courage to live my truth. This energy of God's love empowered me.

The closing ceremony at the retreat was a farewell to my soul family. We all stated in prayer and intention that we would have the next retreat in Hawaii. Yes, I wanted to be there to continue this journey with the ones I am connected with. Ever since I was a child, I'd had dreamt of going to Hawaii. Now I wanted to go there with this group and somehow, I knew, it would be manifested.

Back home in Florida, my life was changing. I was feeling more disconnected from my husband. I was creating more and more separation in our marriage. I began reading Gary Zukav's book, *Seat of the Soul*. Every word moved me into being more conscious. I knew deep down in my heart I had to either choose to stay in my marriage or to leave it, but I wanted to make a responsible, conscious choice. As Gary writes in his book:

"*A responsible choice is a choice that takes into account the consequences of each of your choices. In order to make a responsible choice you must ask yourself, for each choice that you are considering,*

'*What will this produce?*'

'*Do I really want to create that?*'

'*Am I ready to accept all of the consequences of this choice?*'

"*Project yourself into the probable future that will unfold with each choice that you are considering. Do this not with the energy of intention, but simply to test the water, to get the feel for what you are considering creating. See how you feel. Ask yourself, 'Is this what I really want?' and then decide. When you take the consequences of your choice into your decision and when you choose to remain conscious, that is a responsible choice.*"[12]

I appreciated my friendship with Gary. When I would phone him crying and afraid, he would hold the space for me as I shared my fears. I wanted to make a choice from my higher self. I prayed for God to show me the way and was open to receive truth from my guides, angels and teachers. Gary was both a messenger and a teacher for me. His wisdom and knowledge supported me through this challenging time.

The retreat in Hawaii was approaching. I wanted to go, but had no money to pay for it. I wanted to go to find the strength to heal my relationship with my husband or leave it.

One day I received a call from Valerie, a new friend from the Mt. Shasta retreat. She told me she had paid for my retreat, all I had to do was get there. But flights to Hawaii are not cheap, it was Christmas time and there was no extra money to spare. How could I possibly go?

One night in my prayers I told God I had let go of the outcome, but I really wanted to experience the retreat in Hawaii. I became very clear with my intention, saying, "Dear God, I want to go and I want to manifest this trip without having to pay it back. I believe I deserve a gift from the universe if it is in my highest good to be there." When I finished, I was amazed by the feeling of peace that came over me and knew my prayer had been heard. I also felt myself let go of the outcome. If the trip did not come easily then I was not supposed to go.

The next morning, having forgotten my request from the night before, I noticed a light flashing on the message machine. As I listened, I did not recognize the caller. "Frannie, please call me!" said the voice with great urgency. I immediately dialed the unfamiliar number and found to my amazement it was Kim, a man I had been briefly married to when I was twenty-two. We had not spoken for years. Kim said he had called because in his dream God had spoken and told him to. "You know I don't believe too much in that stuff," he said, "but it was so clear for me to call you. So I listened." He was so glad I had returned his call, as I told him about my life at the moment and my difficulty in my marriage. He was very compassionate. Then he told me about a girl in Hawaii he was dating. Somewhere in there I mentioned in passing that I wanted to go to Hawaii for a retreat, but could not afford the airfare.

Not putting it all together until later, I was totally surprised when he said, "Please let me take care of your flight, it's the least I could do." He said he had a lot of guilt around how he had treated me and this would be something he could give me now. "I have so many frequent-flyer points that I must use up by January and I'll just lose them if I don't use them," he explained.

Wow! What a gift! I was so grateful he listened to God's voice in his dream. I booked a first-class ticket to Hawaii that day and arranged for Luke and Lane to stay with my parents because Bob was very busy with work.

Going to Hawaii helped to further change my life. Like the fires of the volcano of Pele, I had activated the holy fire of Soul. Now I was to experience the false self, which I would then choose to embrace and love. This was my co-dependent nature that had forgotten how to say no; the self I had previously given to another's vision. There in Hawaii I found the purest love with the earth of the island and with the dolphins. And there I met two people who moved me into an even greater knowing of myself.

These two people reflected for me true love in their commitment to self and to their relationship. Their names are Ewa (who now calls herself Freedom) and Todd. We had an instant connection and I felt very at home with them. After the retreat in Hawaii ended, I wasn't yet ready to go back to the world I had left behind, so they invited me to stay with them. There was more for me to experience as soul, here in Hawaii.

During the retreat I roomed with two women, Kristine and Theresa. We became three peas in a pod. Their support was so unconditional. They left me in Hawaii as I courageously stayed to face my greatest fears. Intuitively I knew this was what I needed to do, to anchor my new way of being. When we said our goodbyes, Kristine handed me a card along with money to support me in staying. God once told me there would be angels in bodies, helping me to stay here to bring the message of love to the world. For me she is definitely one of them.

I stayed in Hawaii for another week with Ewa and Todd. They lived consciously and by being with them I met the part of myself that chose to live consciously, too; the part of myself committed to healing. They were gourmet vegetarian chefs. I learned how to make healthy food even more delicious. With them, I became more conscious in my eating, my breathing and more conscious in my being.

Almost every day we would kayak out to the pods of wild dolphins, who would then join us in their territory. Watching Todd in the water was like watching a dolphin. At first I was afraid, but soon I learned to let go with my new dolphin friends and began to feel the great love of these amazing creatures.

Ewa and Todd had taken some intense workshops on healing codependency. It wasn't easy to be with them at times, because of the intensity of their intimacy. There was nothing covering them up. I remember one of the first things Todd said to me was, "Why are you smiling so much?" He was feeling his hurt and pain from past wounds and found it hard to trust my happiness. While it was often difficult to be with them, it moved me to question the false masks I wear to cover my own pain. The pain I learned to cover up so well with a smile. For all those years I modeled, I learned very well how to dress up for the unconscious world around me.

We meditated together. We cooked together. We danced together. We prayed together. We broke bread together. We released our emotions together. Together, we allowed the breath to move us deeper into unknown places of self.

It was often a very uncomfortable place to be. I was questioned a lot for my behavior and I didn't always like that. I wanted to run back to the safety of my old world. But, intuitively I knew why I was there. On our Spiritual quest we may move into dark places, or to extreme behaviors to bring us into balance. Maybe that is why I was there. I was beginning to understand the words my sister Philomene's shaman teacher, Oriah Mountain Dreamer, wrote in a poem called, "The Invitation":

> *"It doesn't interest me if this story you tell me is true. I want to know if you can disappoint another to be true to yourself; if you can bear the accusations of betrayal and not betray your soul; if you can be faithless and therefore trustworthy."*[13]

I was remembering how to be true to myself, even if my answers made other people uncomfortable. Perhaps the experience was out of balance, but I knew at home I was out of balance as a codependent caretaker. I needed to experience and to free the other side of myself.

My experience with the dolphins opened my heart to joy in my Self. I loved being in the sea, feeling the water embrace me. Under the water I could hear the song of the dolphins. They jumped over us, spiraling around us. Looking into their eyes deepened me to feel a love I had never known in this world. I felt they were speaking to me and hearing my own song.

After swimming, we would sit on the beach and eat coconuts, strawberry papayas, macadamia nuts and bananas. The earth supported our healing. There was nothing to hide being with these dolphin people. They showed me how to touch myself with compassion; to live authentically and freely. I did not like who I was at times – a frightened little girl who wanted love. But I came to realize that no one could give me love until I freed my self from my own fears. Here in Hawaii I was connecting with my fears, yet I was allowing my soul self to take charge. I wanted to stay here. I was afraid to go home to Florida. I was different now. I felt empowered in some ways, but was afraid I might lose myself the moment I stepped into my old life again. I was learning to take care of my little girl inside.

On the flight back to Tampa, I fell asleep and had a dream: I arrived back in Tampa with no baggage. There was no one to pick me up, but a car was waiting for me. I got into the car and drove myself home. In the car there was a cell phone ringing. I picked it up and a woman named Gerri was on the phone saying, "Where have you been, don't you know I need you?"

I said, "I am just arriving home. I need to take care of myself right now. I have to give to myself and set some boundaries here. I will call you when I am available to give to you." The plane landed and I woke up.

The moment I walked into my house, the phone rang. It was Gerri. The dream had been the dress rehearsal and the conversation began, "Frannie, where have you been? I need you..."

I spoke my truth. Gerri represented my own needy child. I set her free by taking care of myself. Gerri was an intricate part of healing my own codependency. I could not give to anyone but myself right then. Maybe at the time it created a great deal of pain and separation for Gerri, but we are still dear friends and both of us have grown in the love of self. It was time for both of us to accept our womanhood and to make choices, freeing the needy child.

18

With Love We Have the Courage to Listen and the Courage to Speak

I began facilitating meditation groups in Englewood. The Women's Development Center asked me to start a few sessions and I was excited to be of service after such a long interval of aloneness. I was eager to share what I had learned about healing body, mind and Spirit. I was still very cautious of going out into the world of perfumes and toxic environments, yet I was called to share the energy and truth of God in me; to share all I had learned about nutrition, stillness of mind, mindfulness, inner child work, dream interpretation, yoga, emotional work, breath work and so much more. I believe we teach what we are here to learn and the women in my groups were starving to experience this part of Self.

The first evening of a six-week meditation group arrived and I was excited and nervous at the same time. I prepared some handouts, but mostly I wanted the evening's session to be time for the women to put energy into themselves. I gifted them with information I had learned, but the real treasure was the opportunity to have a safe place where they could share their hearts and pain without judgment. We were all on a journey to know self and I recognized the courage it took for each woman to share her own story.

I led them in a guided meditation to find that stillness within where we can hear God speak, to that place where we can meet our guides, angels and spirit loved ones in our open hearts – the bridge between the worlds. The energy of two or more gathered is beautiful and the intimacy of hearts opened was a safe place for all to be vulnerable and reveal our truths.

Codependency was a big issue and the circle allowed each one present to share information from which we all could grow. As the facilitator, I brought a way of healing and felt opened by everyone else's experiences. It was a beautiful evening as I let God guide me moment by moment.

During the meditation I saw a man in soul body stand beside Terry, one of the participants. This being wanted me to bring a message to her; but I was not sure if I was ready to let these women know about my gift of hearing communication from the other side. Perhaps I was afraid I would not be accepted, or maybe I doubted my gift. I wanted these women to trust me first, so I said to Spirit if the opportunity opened for me to feel safe in revealing what I had seen, I would tell her. Today, I'm no longer like this. I know the messages are for all of us, yet if the person is not open, it may shut them down more. I have learned patience, because God always shows me the way.

I like how Wayne Dyer, in his book *10 Secrets For Success And Inner Peace*, expressed it:

"In form, you receive *in-formation*.

When you move to spirit, you receive *Inspiration*." [14]

After the group ended I watched the women leave as I emptied cups and moved the chairs back into place. I was disappointed I had not had the right opportunity to speak to Terry, when suddenly the door opened and she came back in. "I just wanted to make sure you have the key to lock up," she said.   Here was my opportunity. I invited her to sit down with me and then I shared my experience.

"Terry," I said, "During the meditation, your father was standing right beside you and wanted me to relay a message to you." Her eyes filled with tears and they began rolling down her cheeks. She was overcome emotionally to know that her father was with her in Spirit. As we sat together quietly, I closed my eyes and pictures came to my mind as I spoke the words I felt.

First I saw a little girl opening the door of a bedroom where a baby cousin was sleeping. The little girl was excited and picked up the baby. Then she twirled him around, accidentally bumping the baby's head on the wall. She was suddenly afraid and put the baby back in the crib. Not long after, the baby died of a brain tumor.

Terry told me she was the little girl in my vision. Later she shared with me that her own daughter had also died of a brain tumor at a very young age. She had always believed God had taken her daughter to punish her for the accident that happened when she was a child. Her father had come to tell her she did not kill her cousin. She was neither condemned as guilty, nor was God punishing her.

Can you imagine holding that memory, that false belief of guilt, for almost fifty years? Terry now sat before me in tears, knowing I spoke the truth. She had never told anyone what had happened all those years ago. She had carried the guilty secret alone for all those years. This message from her father could finally free her from that guilt. In that moment I witnessed the weight lifting from her heart as she finally realized the truth of her innocence. It was beautiful to watch. It also brought a truth to me. I realized I was to use this gift to bring truth to those who might have no other way of finding it.

We each have gifts that we came into this world to share. By doing our inner work and listening to our own self in Spirit, we can lift the veil of separation and communicate with the other side. I believe we are all telepathic, to the extent that we are open to each other. But too many of us are hiding the truth, by hiding the darkness. I believe we can all become masters and allow our energy fields to be open and vast to receive and give information. Our energy always tells the truth. When we connect with the love within, we will have the courage to listen and then we will have the courage to speak.

19

Why Didn't The Dream Live?

The choices I made in my life may not have seemed right to another's eyes, but the experiences that resulted showed me my truth at the time. This long period of healing and self-discovery was most difficult for my husband Bob. One day he told me he knew he had to set me free. He said my wings had been broken, but now I was ready to fly again. He let me go with love. Life had become an adventure to discover more of myself. We are all free in our own hearts and the birdcage I was in had always been open through my own heart. I was free to fly – if I chose to.

The decision to leave my marriage was the most difficult choice I have ever made. Life didn't become easier by any means. The journey deeper into myself just continued without my spouse. But I found a partner inside of me, my Self. I was beginning to embrace the Beloved in me.

Many months after our separation, I invited Bob to have Easter dinner with us. It was a very uncomfortable evening. When I walked him to the door after dinner, my body was filled with so many feelings. Later that night I wrote in my journal to help me express what was going on inside of me:

April 6, 1995 (Excerpt from my journal)
My body speaks to me...
> *of memories so deep within my cells.*
I held my emotions in my body...
> *feeling withdrawn.*
Able to do the skills of cooking dinner and serving it.
Then he left... soon after dinner.
I walked with my body in a way not knowing...
I held the space as I began to feel so many emotions...

which one wanted to reign?
There was no guilt, that's a switch.
It was all then embraced by Philomene's phone call
          as she spoke the words of my soul... she knew.
All I had to say was that I was feeling so much...
          sadness, anxiety, helplessness, hopelessness, grieving.
She talked... continuing to bring the truth from my cells.
I felt I would explode with emotion.
Now I feel it in my chest...
          my body holding memory.
All the truths never spoken.
Living in the world so close to the surface because,
if it got too intimate, the pain would be
so great...
so great...
so great...
A part of me wants to run and grab him
and hold his inner child that is so lost.
That's the mother in me.
Another part of me wants to grab him
and say the words of the angry one that's inside.
Why couldn't the dream live?
I can't be in that old illusion.
Tonight was reliving the pain and loneliness again.
When will I be able to be free of it?
The cells do hold memory...
It was the beginning of the new me...
the resurrected one.
I am truly free.
I grieve the years of loving this man...
trying to be a family...
A woman who didn't know herself.
I am longing to live now...
Being alone is nice... sweet pain.
I remember our touch... when did it stop feeling good?

"Why?" Lane asks... "I don't understand?" she asks.
I speak little words with great understanding.
I cry and she says she understands.
Do I blame Bob? Sometimes...
I do blame me... sometimes.
Two souls moving away...
            separately to find oneself.
The children are happy...
We are trying to be friends, Bob and I.
But friends can speak from the heart.
Right now it doesn't feel safe
for if I speak... he may run
and if he speaks... I may hide.
The grief is so deep...
Onion layers to heal the pain.
I cry again... when will I stop crying?
Lane says, "I don't understand."
My little girl says, "I don't understand."

20

Leap of Faith

When I left my marriage, I couldn't work because of my chemical sensitivities and as a Canadian, I didn't have the proper visa to work in the USA. I didn't know how I would support my children and myself. I was getting some money from Bob for child support, but it wasn't enough to live on. Modeling had enabled me to make a lot of money, but I had left modeling far behind me. My decision to leave my marriage brought me to trust and faith; I had to allow myself to be supported by the universe as I searched to find my work.

To do this, I had to learn to let people know what I needed – to speak out in order to be heard. I had to find the courage within to create my life – to speak out and tell the truth of where I was in order to get the support I needed.

This is where I took the leap of faith, not knowing what would happen to me. I meditated and prayed that something would show up. I took care of my needs as best I could. I told people the truth of where I was and trusted the messenger would come.

When we step into the truth of who we really are, we then have the knowing that our faith in God and Self will be enough. We may not know in the moment how it will happen, or when it will come, but as we step into the space of faith, we know our 'good' can come from anyone, or anything.

Before, I thought support would come from my husband or my job. I had the expectation that my 'good' was going to come from that which I thought was my source. However, when the source is not a human source, but rather the Divine Source, anyone can be the messenger bringing what is needed. You just have to be open to whatever is coming and have faith that something or someone will arrive as your supply.

It is a very different way of living. All my sources of previously perceived security had been shattered. The Source within, this great flow of love, urged me to speak and to be heard. With love, we have the courage to speak.

Bob and I were still living in the same house, when one day I prayed to God, the angels and my guides for help in selling the house, so we could both move forward. I felt myself letting go as I went to sleep.

It was very early the next morning when the phone rang. The man's voice was clear but one I didn't recognize. He said, "Frannie, I am your neighbor two doors down and I wondered if you and your husband would be interested in trading homes. Our home might be easier to sell because it is smaller." I told him that Bob was in Canada and I would call him back later.

I got off the phone knowing that my prayer had been answered. We traded homes and Luke, Lane and I moved into the home two doors down and Bob moved into one of the apartments that we owned. I guess the timing was right; we were both ready to let go. The kids and I lived in the house while it was up for sale. The next summer I drove with them back to Ontario for a visit. While we were there, the house finally sold and I had two weeks to find a new place to live. This was the beginning of truly being on my own without Bob.

I didn't rush right back because I trusted that the perfect house was there waiting for us to move into. I called a realtor and all he could show me were two-bedroom homes or five and six-bedroom homes. I wanted something bigger than a two-bedroom home, so we could all have our own bedrooms.

The realtor said he had a five-bedroom place for rent on the Gulf of Mexico. I hesitated, but then thought, "What the heck! Let's look." We walked in and Lane and Luke both found their bedrooms right away. The rent was $1500 a month. All I had to start my new life was three thousand dollars in the bank. I was getting some child support and my meditation classes were bringing me a little money. How could I do it?

I went to church the next day and heard Rev. David Owen Ritz say, "Know what you want, then take a leap of faith, trust that you are taken care of."

So I went back to the house, praying for a sign to guide me. As I walked to the front door, I found an eagle feather on the ground. I felt it was a sign for me. Then I walked to the rocks at the edge of the water. I had truth chills running up and down my spine. "God, give me another sign," I asked, " I'm afraid to make a mistake." Just then a dolphin leaped out of the water right in front of me! I felt the joy rise up in me as I said, "Yes!" to myself. "Yes," I heard inside, "this is not a house just for you. This is a home for many to gather. This house will be for many."

Talk about taking a risk. I thought about it and then called the realtor and asked him to offer the owner $1,200 a month. He called back to say the owner had accepted!

What I really wanted to pay was between $600 - 800 a month. This house was double that, but I saw the bigger picture. This would be a place where I could work. I would do my group meditations and healing circles here. I would facilitate A *Course in Miracles* group and I would do my spiritual counseling with those who wanted private sessions.

I would have weekend retreats and open this house up as a healing center. I was inspired and I was feeling alive again. The donations I would receive would help me with my rent and to support my family.

The day after I signed the lease, the realtor called and asked if I would be willing to rent out the house in February, for one month, for five thousand dollars. Amazing! For that month we could move to my parents' home nearby and over the next year, that five thousand dollars would bring my rent down to what I wanted to pay in the beginning.

By the time February came, I was making enough money to pay the rent. I had groups almost every day of the week and the evenings Luke and Lane spent with their father.

The number of women and men attending my groups grew in number. I facilitated weekend Goddess retreats and my work supported me. Everything I was doing was helping others, but it was also for me. I loved creating these sacred spaces for people to heal and to discover the truth about themselves. All I was learning for myself, I shared with others.

One morning, I woke up remembering a dream in which I was told I would meet a new teacher. A few days later, I got a call from a woman who asked if I would counsel her ten-year-old grandson. When Joan arrived with her grandson, Eric, I first talked with both of them together. Joan talked about Eric without reservations, telling me his difficulties going to public school because he could see and feel energy. As a result, he had a very difficult time being in the world. He was usually happier playing alone, or inventing things. He had strong relationships with animals and nature, as these provided a safe place for him.

His grandmother told me that when she first began to raise him, he did not read or write and had no religious education of any sort. Yet he spoke about spiritual matters as if he had studied for years. Where did all this information come from? He did not have parents or peers around him talking about God or energy, yet this young boy spoke about the Universal truths as naturally as most boys his age talked about building forts or playing baseball.

I sat alone with him and let him just share with me. Where did all this information come from if no one taught it to him? He talked to me about energy and we shared as if we were long lost friends coming together to talk about spiritual experiences – just as I usually do with like-minded people.

The first time I took him through a meditation, I put my hands on the areas of his body that related to the chakras and he then told me the colors he was seeing. I could feel the blocks in these areas of his body where he was holding memories of a traumatic childhood. I guided Eric to a place where he could release his hurt and pains by seeing them as rocks he could lift out of himself. I also showed him how he could be with his fears without leaving his body, or going into his mind. He participated openly and I saw how much he wanted to let go of these anxieties inside of him.

Then we went beyond this world together and he connected with his guardian angel. Together on the bridge between the worlds, I allowed Spirit to speak as I felt the presence move into both of us. It was the energy of Archangel Michael and it surrounded us with light. "You are the receiver, Eric," said the voice clearly and directly.

Each session I had with Eric taught me that truth comes for us if we are open to receiving it. He is a gifted, young boy who is learning to live in the world with the high spiritual knowledge that we are energy. His intelligence is natural because it is connected with the intelligence of God. He has difficulty with the academic world, yet with love and support around him, he has found his way to be Eric.

Eric is now in high school and his grandmother has written a book about her experiences with him. She told me the work I did with Eric, which focused on helping him embrace his fears and release his hurt, helped him to integrate into the world more easily and to be more present and focused.

The book is called *The Receiver. Conversations With Eric.*

21

Take Off Your Shoes
You Don't Have To Die

I never read Elizabeth Kubler-Ross' books until years after Debbie's death. It happened like this. One day I found Kubler-Ross' book, *Death and Dying*, in a bag underneath some other books I had. Where had this book come from, I wondered? The next morning I awoke very early as the wind blew my door open and slammed it against the wall. And then I felt Debbie's presence, so strongly, sitting on my bedside. I heard her so clearly that I began talking to her, as if she were there in her body.

She encouraged me to get my book written and into the world. I had been writing for years, but daily survival seemed to take up so much of my energy. My physical health was still challenged by chemical exposure. She told me it was now time for me to move fully into the world. To step into my purpose, my reason for being here. She assured me it was time and to trust in the opportunities. I remember saying, "But I need help."

I felt her more alive there with me than ever before. The energy I was feeling and the truth I was hearing opened me. I, too, had fears of dying that surfaced when I had no energy to go on, when I was sick.

Suddenly, I felt a strong desire to read the book Debbie had wanted me to read before her death. It was 5:30 am, but I opened it and immediately began reading. When I finally finished it later that morning, I went to see my girlfriend Chris, who was visiting from New York. I asked her if she was interested in helping me bring my work into the world. Without hesitating, she said yes. We decided right then she would come live with us. I was also facilitating a Goddess retreat that weekend and I chose death and dying as the main theme.

Lane, who was now ten, came home after being away that weekend, with questions about birth and death. I held the space for her questioning mind. When I told her the story of Debbie's death, she burst into hysterical tears. She was afraid that because I had just read, *Death and Dying,* now I would die like Debbie had. And if I died, then where would I be? She was very scared. She said she'd have to hold me all night to keep me in my body. I assured her I was not going to die, but I understood how she felt. I took her into bed with me and we held each other until she fell asleep. After she was asleep, I turned on the light to read and meditate.

A few hours later I turned off the light and was just about to close my eyes when Lane sat up in her sleep and said, "Mommy, take off your shoes, you don't have to die." The light in the darkened room suddenly became very bright and my body felt like it was on fire. A wonderful peace filled and then expanded my heart, as Lane crawled back under the covers and back into the unconscious dream-state. Excitement coursed through my whole body. Those nine words went straight into me and filled me with inspiration. They reflected to me the truth of Soul living in the physical body. In that moment, I let go of the false self, the artificial coverings, to feel who I truly was. It was only the false self that was dying - I, the true Frannie, was not dying at all. I was letting go of the fear to let the love in. Allowing myself to be real and authentic.

There is no doubt in me that Debbie was there in the Soul body with Lane and me that night. I felt it in my heart. But it wasn't until years later, when I visited with Debbie's sister Cely, that I made the connection. Following our visit, Cely sent me an e-mail that brought back memories of Debbie's obsession with her feet.

In high school, shoes were very important to Debbie - how they looked; how they felt. Now here she was, telling me through my daughter, "Take off your shoes, you don't have to die!"

In the moments I was holding Lane before she fell asleep, when she was afraid I was going to die - I felt God's perfection on many levels. This embrace symbolized the Spiritual adult holding the wounded child. Through the love of the adult, the child is able to let go of fear so she feels safe and empowered.

There is wholeness in the psyche when these parts within us are together. Sometimes the Spiritual adult is running around saying, "I can do this," and "I can do that," while the frightened little child inside is throwing a tantrum, just wanting to be loved and held. When the Spiritual adult holds the wounded child, the Spiritual adult gets real and the wounded child gets healed. Then we have authenticity of Self and wholeness in the psyche. We can hold the space for others who come to us wounded, in fear and calling for love. We understand them. We may not always be successful in holding the space, for as long as we are having this human experience, people will push our buttons. But we will be more open to others because we have the experience and they may sense that we have gone through it, too!

The biggest fear I had in the past was if I became my true self, I would lose the love. But unless we become ourselves, we are never going to gain the love, which doesn't die. We may not know what that means, but we can still experience truth of love – a deathless, unconditional love. The only way to do it is to surrender the conditions. When we stop trying to get people to love us and instead choose to love ourselves, then we will be able to include others in that love. That is unconditional love. Then we truly have it, for that love never dies.

In that moment when Lane was in fear, I knew it wasn't true, but I did not judge or invalidate her. I accepted where she was and she felt my unconditional love. I let her sleep with me and did not abandon her. I gave to the child and in doing so, I gave to myself.

Out of the mouths of babes the truth does come. I held the space for Lane as she allowed her fears to surface. I did not stop the flow of Holy Spirit moving into her life. When she sat up in that flow, in the power of truth, she told me not to be afraid. She taught me to be real and empowered me with her own self-love. As I see it now, she was the mirror of my own little girl self. I allowed them – Lane and Little Frannie – to be, not judging them. I held them in love and in that love I created a space for my own empowerment.

This is what Debbie did for me with her death; she held the space for me as Soul, allowing me to find out who I was. Allowing me to give myself the same love so I could hold Lane in love for her own truth to emerge. Lane's truth is my truth: to let each other be in fear without judgment. As I held Lane in love, I held my own fear in unconditional love. How could I ever help the world if I judged my own self?

What has to die is the false self. That's what Debbie did the night before she died. As her mother held her, she faced her false self, the one with the fears, the one that lied, the one afraid of judgment. Releasing her shadow by holding herself in her own heart, allowed her to see the truth of herself.

The false self must ultimately die before the true self can be reborn. This is what Jesus meant when he said, "Lest you die, you cannot be reborn." The truth simply cannot be born until the parts that are not true, die.

We have to learn to stand alone. Learning this was an important life lesson for me. Standing alone is not the end of the journey, but rather its very center. We must recognize that others have their own experiences and their own beliefs and they cannot define our lives for us. Sometimes we have to separate from them to find out what we are all about. This is a normal and healthy part of growth.

This is what happens when kids leave home. They have to find out who they are. In the context of the whole experience of their lives, separation is a very important part. To truly grow up and learn who we are, we have to learn to stand alone.

Most people are afraid of standing alone because they fear standing alone may mean NO LOVE. But standing alone means SELF LOVE. When you stand alone you learn to love yourself and then you can stand with others as equals. When you are living on another's terms, you'll never be equal.

Many of us are afraid to find out who we are, because we fear if we do, no one will love us. When I came into the world, I arrived as one of triplets. I realized in this incarnation, perhaps unconsciously, that I needed to separate from my sisters to find out who I was. Although there was comfort in being one of three, I knew I needed to stand alone as an individual. Not easy to do when your mother dresses you alike and you are all in the same class.

Frannie   Philomene   Colleen

I don't think my mother actually realized what was going on until we came home for lunch on our first day of school. We told her that morning we had been photographed, filmed and interviewed by newspaper and T.V. reporters. I had felt threatened by all the commotion, away from the safety of home. We were fresh to this new world; at least that's how I felt. We were different and a lot of attention was focused on us. After that first morning our mom realized we needed to have our own identities and never dressed us alike again.

But how could I separate from my sisters and still feel the closeness and love I so desperately wanted? Somehow I felt it just wasn't a good thing to leave them.

As an adult, my sister Colleen and her friend Charlotte started a cosmetic and skincare company in Canada called Goldlinx. When they expanded into the United States, Colleen asked me to be spokesperson, since her product line was created for and inspired by my challenges with chemicals. With my modeling background, I could bring Goldlinx a lot of experience. Our main market in the US was modeling schools.

So I began traveling again. I had a monthly retainer and was paid for my work when I traveled to cities in the United States. I began to move myself into the world again. I was different now and was inspired to do it differently. The monthly paycheck was such a gift and being with Colleen again was a dream come true. We loved being in a hotel room together at night, sharing just like we did as little girls. This was a very special time with my sister and I loved it.

Being grown-up identical twins, we began attracting a lot of attention in the industry. Now we saw the gift of being two women more alike than most could be; yet our differences were shining from within. One cell split in two. Now, as an adult, I didn't care if people could tell us apart. I knew who I was and so did Colleen. The years of separation had allowed each of us to grow and develop our own identity.

Philomene   Frannie   Colleen

22

To Live Life In A Lighter Way

*It is in the living moment of the now that seeds are planted
and every future holds the energy of its birth.*

My brother's partner, Marion, was diagnosed with cancer on
Thursday November 14, 1996. Three days later, she died. The
experience was shocking to our whole family and I cannot imagine
the impact it had on my brother Phil. They had a beautiful
relationship and he was very committed to her. Even in the pain
of healing past issues, they shared a strong love and friendship.

I liked Marion as a person and enjoyed our relationship,
especially early on, when she and Phil first met. I felt such a
connection with her. I was experiencing the onset of EI
(Environmental Illness) and Marion had Chronic Fatigue Syndrome.
We shared a mutual understanding of the required diet and lifestyle
changes. We had much in common in our illnesses and our abilities
to touch our emotions and wounds. Her energy sometimes
intimidated me and her commitment to truth sometimes pushed
me deeper into my own wounds, yet we shared a love I will always
have.

She taught me to speak up for my needs and my convictions.
Whether she was aware of it or not, she was a remarkable teacher.
At times it was difficult for me to feel close to her, but I felt Marion
open more to me again near her death. It felt good. Her dying
brought so much to me and I miss her in so many ways.

Often I think of Marion and speak to her from my heart. Almost
a year after her death, I wondered why she still had not come to
me in Spirit. I had not yet actually felt her presence except in my
thoughts. This challenged my fear about my relationship with
Spirit and raised doubts about my gift to communicate with Souls
beyond the physical plane.

One evening I sat in meditation and strongly felt a presence in the room – it was Marion. I was surprised that I felt fear in being with her because I knew her as a sister and a friend. Maybe I was experiencing what others feel when they fear death. I just couldn't go to that place where I could receive her. I was afraid and the fear shut my heart, but I did not judge my feelings. Instead, I asked her to come to me in a dream that night.

The morning came and I remembered my dream and her message to me was to trust Spirit. She wanted me to trust the experience.

I had an appointment that morning, but the woman called and canceled. I decided instead to sit in silence and almost immediately I felt Marion's presence. In my minds eye I saw her sit before me. She felt joyous and full of love and happiness. She looked younger, like she was when I first met her. She turned her head to the side and her hair fell softly over her eye. It was so real. Her smile was so free.

This time I felt no fear at all. It was just as if I were sitting cross-legged on the floor with my dear sister, sharing. My intuition told me to pick up a pen and write. The words came through as a letter to her partner, my brother, Phil. I also knew the message was for me and anyone else who reads it. The words I share with you now and the gift of her gentle Spirit, brings truth:

October 21ˢᵗ, 1997

My Dearest Phil,

It is so much easier without my tired body. I was so tired of the pain of living in harmony with what I believed was true. There was always so much to do and my mind had so much information. It is easy now to see the truth. Live life in a lighter way. Don't take life so seriously. Laughing is the greatest gift we can give to ourselves. I know it is hard now to feel the joy of life. But like everything, there is a season to withdraw and there is a season to rejoice in living. Fall seems like the time to withdraw inside, but it is good to touch your insides with a huge belly laugh. It stirs things up really good and soon the part of you that seeded truth a long time ago will birth its beautiful fruit. Do you know that I birthed a lot even without physically living there in a body with you? Humans forget about the way of creation. It is in the living moment of the now that seeds are planted and every future holds the energy of its birth. I felt my self-worth the moment I let go of the heavy body. I moved into the truth that only the light could show me. My darkness and life was the hard shell, or maybe you could say, the womb for my fruits. It is all part of the world now and I am always a part of that creation.

I sit here cross-legged in celebration of Spirit life and I know through our love you will birth your creations while still in your physical body.

I am with you always Phil and I am in joy of your open heart. I touch you here and I know we are always connected and growing to be who we are. You are body and flesh and me in light and love. I am free now of all the limits I put on myself in body. I am free and I can be all that I am.

Feel me in your creations, for we are partners to bring more light to this earth.

I am always loving you, Marion

The words spoke to me. Maybe my fear was to birth my seeds. I felt the shell of my false self. Afraid to be me. This book is a seed I wanted to birth. I am allowing these parts of me to be shared. I don't have to be right; I just have to be my truth. These experiences have brought me to the truth of who I am. Love is shared.

When I sent this letter to Phil, he told me that just the night before, he had done yoga for the first time since Marion's death. They used to do yoga together and near her death, she was in such pain she had trouble sitting in certain positions. Phil thought this was why she said in her letter, "I sit here cross-legged in celebration of Spirit life..." He told me he had set out her mat beside his, as if he were joining her in doing their yoga exercises. He also told me that the thesis she had been working on for her doctorate had some of the same message I had received from Marion. It was his way of acknowledging the gift she gave to both of us that day. She's OK and so are we.

Marion had so much pain. I understood because I have had great pain too and I can easily stay in that place when I am in my mind. In the same way Marion says, "I moved into the truth that only the light can show me," my own heart shows me the way to the light. I can then laugh from my belly and see how life need not be so heavy. I can appreciate the humor of this life's lessons. Laughing is the greatest gift I can give to myself and those around me. Sometimes I am too serious and I love it when I can break that pattern and just let go and laugh with whoever I am with.

Marion had a quick wit. I admired it and maybe it was another part of herself that wanted to heal the pain. Maybe we are all afraid of our own light. Marion was a big light on this planet and she shines in many hearts as she continues to create with all that she touched. She continues to be a source of inspiration for me. God bless our soul family and friends who bring us to self.

As Nelson Mandela said at his 1994 Inaugural Speech:

"Our deepest fear is not that we are inadequate.
Our deepest fear is that we are powerful beyond measure.
It is our Light, not our Darkness, that most frightens us.
We ask ourselves, who am I to be brilliant, gorgeous, talented, fabulous?
Actually, who are you not to be?
You are a child of God. Your playing small does not serve the world.
There is nothing enlightened about shrinking so that other people won't feel insecure around you.
We were born to make manifest the Glory of God that is within us.
It is not just in some of us; it is in everyone.
And as we let our Light shine, we unconsciously give other people permission to do the same.
As we are liberated from our own fear, our presence automatically liberates others."[15]

Did Marion know how bright her light was? I hope she is reading these words with me. Of course she is... she is the words I write. To affirm our own light we must break through our darkness or false self with love. Many who have died have brought this message to me in one way or another.

23

Bliss Is Letting Go

After my fourteen-year marriage to Bob ended, I slowly began to date. I thought I was looking for the man that would join with me on a Spiritual journey through life. I discovered that just as my illness had been a catalyst for my own healing, my relationships with men also moved me even further towards myself. Each new man was another opportunity to meet parts of myself that I was longing to know, but had not yet met. Each relationship brought me to that needy little girl inside that did not feel loved. These men also inspired me to feel my creative force and the joy of being in a body.

The men I attracted were all committed to a Spiritual path, yet it seemed to me they were unavailable. Looking back I see that I attracted exactly what I was - not available. My neediness was painfully evident as each relationship ended; yet the pain always brought me to more of my own evolution as soul. I learned I needed to commit more fully to my own desires for love and partnership within my self.

Somehow, I continued to create abandonment in my associations with men. I had been dating one man and the relationship ended the day we planned on going to Key West to finally have some quality time together. What I felt was a desire to move more deeply into our relationship, but the whole idea seemed to produce fear for him. My passion for commitment pushed him further away. Being committed to myself helped me realize that this relationship wasn't what I wanted.

I decided to go anyway, to lick my wounds and try to understand why this was happening to me again. I called Joy and invited her to come with me. Her immediate response was, "Yes!" By the time I arrived at Joy's house, I had thought of another destination. The Temple of the Universe in Alachua, near Gainesville, Florida was the same distance from Englewood, but north instead of south. I had heard about this beautiful Hindu/ Buddhist temple and wanted to experience the energy there. I decided to flip a coin, since God is in coins too, and the coin told us to head north to Alachua. I trusted. I had packed for the south, but was open to Alachua. I was happy to be on my way to somewhere.

Traveling with Joy is always a delight. We both giggle and laugh like children and our support and love for one another is truly unconditional. Joy has always been a wonderful reflection, allowing me to hear myself and understand my life experiences in her presence. We have known each other for more than a decade and even though she's almost my mother's age, our friendship is not defined by our age difference. I am the 'child of her heart' and her daughter, Mary, is just like a sister to me. Mary had the same challenge as I did with chronic fatigue and chemical sensitivities.

My heart was broken once again, but I believed much truth and insight would come out of my willingness to see myself; to look within and without to reveal unspoken mysteries. Even though I was with a companion, I was still with myself and my silence continued to show the true face of God in me.

We found a perfect hotel room near the Temple, then we were off to discover and uncover. The Temple was surrounded by many acres of trees and open space and the land was healing unto itself. The air was clear and pure, unlike the air back home on Manasota Key where I lived, which had been tarnished for some weeks with the irritating stench of red tide. Here in Alachua, it was a relief for my lungs to once again be feeling the fullness of my breath.

As we entered the quiet of the Temple, a candle burned on an altar ordained with the pictures of the masters of many religions and Spiritual practices. This was truly a sacred place to feel the arms of Mother God wrapped around me. My meditation moved me to feel my pain and I wept. Joy quoted me a line from a poem she had written: "*Jesus wept and the Buddha cried. There's peace and joy on the other side.*" The tears opened me to deeper places of self where light danced in my heart and the love of divine Spirit touched me sweetly.

Then a presence in Spirit came into my awareness. It felt as if I'd known this presence forever. She spoke to me without words. I heard the words Anandamayi Ma in the silence of my heart. Who was this Presence?

The next day we attended the service, and afterwards I approached someone and asked if she had ever heard the name Anandamayi Ma. Why I picked this person was a mystery, but truly synchronistic. The moment I asked, her eyes widened in amazement. Anandamayi Ma was an Avatar, an East Indian Saint, she told me. She represented bliss to all who met her.

"I live very close by," she said. "If you wait here, I will go home and get some more information about her for you." She drove off, and returned a short while later with a picture along with information about the life of Anandamayi Ma and the ashram she was part of in Hawaii.

This guru, Anandamayi Ma, was one of the greatest saints of the twentieth century. Born in East Bengal (now Bangladesh) in 1896, she influenced the spirituality of thousands, bringing the presence of Bliss to the people who came to see her throughout her long life. Anandamayi Ma died in 1981.

That night I asked Anandamayi Ma to come to me in a dream and show me how to attain bliss. The next morning I woke up remembering my dream. In it, I was driving in my van with Joy and suddenly knew I was going to drive over a cliff and die. I heard the voice of Anandamayi Ma say loudly to me, "If you want to know bliss, let go of all attachments."

A week after our trip to Alachua, my girlfriend Kristine came to visit for a week. We had met at the Mt. Shasta retreat five years earlier. This was a difficult time for me, as my heart was still grieving the loss of not only this relationship but also past relationships. These emotions opened me up to past hurts I hadn't yet healed. One morning I woke up with a very vivid dream, which I shared with Kristine:

I entered the kitchen of my house and my parents were there. My dad was telling me to talk to my friend, Harvey Diamond, and let him know what was going on in my life; to tell him about my break-up with my boyfriend. I then turned and saw Harvey in the corner just smiling. He said, "It's okay, I know all about it."

The dream felt so real. Sometimes dreams feel more real than life itself. I knew that my dream had a message for me, but what was it?

After telling Kristine my dream, we got dressed and went to the church that I sometimes attended. Usually, after services, we met with our friends in the coffee area, but that day I didn't feel up to it. I just didn't want to see anyone. I was still hurting and feeling very vulnerable. I just wanted to hide. We went through the back hallway to slip out, but a few people stopped me. As I looked up and over them, I looked right into the eyes of my friend Harvey.

Then, just like in my dream, he said, "It's okay, I know all about it." He came over and gave me one of his awesome, loving hugs and whispered in my ear that he understood what I was going through; someone had told him of the break-up of my relationship.

I cried in his arms and his compassionate heart touched me. He had just gone through a similar experience. He said, "Frannie, read Paul Ferrini's book, *Love Without Conditions*. His writings have helped me so much, maybe you would like them too."

Well, I believe there are no accidents and my dream told me so. I listened to the messenger and went immediately to buy the book. Months before this happened, a woman in my meditation group had said she wanted me to meet this man, Paul Ferrini, because we were so much alike in the work we do. Laurelie had participated in some of his workshops in Massachusetts and after coming to my workshops and groups, intuitively felt a connection between us would be great. And now I was hearing of Paul Ferrini again from Harvey!

The moment I began to read Paul's words, I felt the truth I was searching for. Every sentence I read reminded me of what I already knew in my heart. It just seems so much more challenging when we are stuck in the emotions of an experience. Slowly I began to forgive and to let go of my attachments to this man who had touched and awakened a place of love within me. I also let go of some feelings and beliefs from my past that I had been afraid to let go of. My dear friend and mentor Paul Ferrini writes in *The Gift of Forgiveness*:

> "God gave you one gift for your journey and one gift alone. He said: 'My son, remember, you can change your mind at any time.'... You can change your mind about every painful and unforgiving thought that you think. You can question each unhappy thought and think another thought that releases you and brings joy into your heart. God did not say, 'I will not let My Son make mistakes.' He said: 'I trust in your return and I give you a gift to see you home.'"[16]

Later that day, Kristine and I went to DeSoto National Memorial, a park in Bradenton, Florida. Even though the red tide was bad, I thought I would be okay, so we took a walk by the seashore. As we drove home that evening, I felt an opening in my heart. I felt the light shining again, from the inside. Turning to

Kristine, I said, "I feel so well right now, I feel I'm letting go." The next deep breath I took, I passed out.

I was lucky Kristine was in the passenger seat. I had been driving slowly, almost at a stand still and she calmly took over the wheel and pulled us to the side of the road. Moments later, I came to, looked at her and said, "I feel fine, I am in bliss." We picked up my son Luke from his friend's house and by the time we got home, my motor activities were slowing down. I seemed to be reacting to something that had hit me hard in my lungs.

Luke remembered what to do. Even though he was pretty young when I'd had severe reactions in the past, he told Kristine to keep walking me around. I began to pass out again and Kristine got nervous and called my mom and dad. By the time they arrived, I had become weaker and was experiencing a flip-flopping in my heart and other unusual symptoms. Everyone was worried and someone decided to call the paramedics. As Lane watched me go into these episodes, she became hysterical. The last time she'd seen this was when she was four or five years old. I'm sure the experience brought a lot of her fears to the surface and she started crying, "Mommy, don't die!"

The paramedics wanted to take me by ambulance to the hospital, but my dad said, "No." He knew if I went to the hospital they would medicate me and he was pretty sure I would not want that. He told them I needed to stay here and that I would be okay.

My dad remembered. He had been present so many times in the past when I'd had severe reactions. This time he was no longer in fear and made a decision from his heart. The episodes slowed down and Lane saw that I would be okay. It used to take days to recover after an experience like that. I could now see it was up to me to connect with my source and let go of the attachments. I had to let go of the false belief that I had to look to someone else – a man – for love. So when the emissions from the red tide hit my lungs, it caused me to react because of my own safety issues. It brought me back to myself. My fear made it worse.

I asked Joy's daughter, Mary to come over, not just because of her friendship, but also because her challenges and experiences with chemical sensitivities were similar to mine. She is a Naturopathic doctor and a hands-on Reiki healer. When she arrived, she took charge (as she would tell you, it's her Capricorn way). A calmness filled the room as she looked into my eyes from her compassionate heart and put her hands on me. Next she brought castor oil packs and laid them on my liver. This remedy which pulls out toxins, has helped me through the years. It is one of the many gifts of the twentieth century mystic Edgar Cayce. Mary knew what to do and I trusted her. Love surrounded me and this gave me strength to heal.

I started to see that the relationships I'd had in the past had conditions for love. Just as these men were afraid of commitment, I was afraid, too! Fears were creating more armor around my heart. I used to project the fear and put blame on the man for having a closed heart and for being afraid to go deeper. I was now free to love deeper and to love myself enough to say that I wanted more in a relationship. I needed to take care of myself and do whatever I needed for my own health and wellness. I know that the pain of losing this relationship broke my heart open to love another more deeply and with more of my true self. I was seeing more clearly that I sabotaged myself for the love of another. I stayed stuck in my past beliefs about myself which closed my heart to love and truth. The toxic environment was a catalyst to help me touch myself in a more loving way.

These relationships were bringing me not only love, but also the parts of myself I was afraid to look at and embrace. They were helping me let go of the attachments I had to something or someone, which I believed could give me the love that I was searching for. I wanted a committed relationship, but first I needed to be committed to my own needs. My little girl inside was growing up. I was choosing to leave another relationship because I knew deep in my heart that I wanted more. My connection to my source continued to inspire me to know that there would be a partner that would be ready to commit and share this life with me.

> *"For now and ever when the love two people share has become the core of their lives, I believe that its power transcends time and space, so deeply placed within, then merges with that which is infinite and silently and surely lives on and on and on..."*
> – Robert Sexton

24

The Dance

I could go into every relationship I've ever had with a man and talk about what went wrong. But each was perfect; each relationship brought me to a greater understanding of what I needed. One day a woman named Jana phoned to try to persuade me to meet Steve, the brother of her best friend. Steve's sister, Sondra, had been urging him to connect with his heart again and heal from his broken marrige.

At that point I had reached a place in my life where I did not want to jump into something I was not ready for. A few months later, she called me again. She told me that Steve just wanted to meet some spiritual friends, so I agreed that he could call me if he wanted. We spoke on the phone a few times and I thought I would invite him to a going away party I was having for my roommate, Chris. Since there would be quite a few single men and women at this gathering, I figured it would not seem like a blind date.

Chris had been living with Lane, Luke and me for three years. We had created a family feeling and Chris supported me personally in so many ways. I didn't yet have the book completed, but she helped me produce meditation tapes and I was busy facilitating workshops. We loved having Chris in our home and in our lives and it was difficult for the children to let her go but Chris and I both knew it was time for her to leave and begin her new life in New Mexico.

On the night of the party, there was a harvest moon. We all met at a restaurant in Sarasota and when Steve walked in, without even knowing what he looked like, I went up to greet him. He was trembling and I could feel his shyness. I had my walls up and I was guarding myself. I didn't want to like this guy. I was tired of all the pain I had experienced with men and I even tried to set him up with one of my girlfriends. At dinner he sat beside me and later we all decided to go dancing.

When Chris and I found ourselves alone for a minute, she looked at me and said, "Frannie, it feels to me like Steve is going to be your life partner."

I was amazed at what she said. The entire time Chris had lived with us, she always had been protective of me, especially regarding the men I dated. Hearing her speak this way told me she clearly had an intuitive knowingness. Still, I felt my resistance to the comment. "How can you say such a thing when you don't even know him and only talked to him for a little while?" I responded.

Then Steve asked me to dance. As I got up to dance with him I felt nervous, but didn't know why. Maybe I was afraid of being seduced again. But as we danced, I let myself relax in his arms and then the fears were gone. The next thing I knew, I suddenly felt safer inside and ready to get to know this man. I remembered my counselor telling me that it takes the love of self to be vulnerable, to go into another relationship after you have been hurt. What I realize now is that we put our rose colored glasses on when we get hooked into a romantic illusion. Yet wouldn't the world be a beautiful place if we all had our rose colored glasses on? After all, our fear-based creations are only illusions anyways; love is the only true reality. A *Course In Miracles* talks about the two real emotions being love and fear. All I knew was that after that dance, after I let my defenses down, I wanted to get to know this man.

This time I found that I was the one holding back in the relationship. There was something inside of me that was not trusting. Was it my past showing up and keeping me in fear of fully loving? Or was it my inner knowing telling me to be cautious because there was something else going on that was not yet evident?

Steve continued to show up and tell me he wanted to be in a committed relationship. When I shared my fears, he would say he was not like the other men I had been with. I would say to myself, Steve is not my past relationships. How could he be? I am different in this moment. When I am in my fears, he can be the mirror of the past that I did not let go of, or he can be the reflection of God's perfect love for me. My inner reality will show me the way.

Still, it was difficult to trust because he was separated but not yet divorced. He told me he was divorced in his heart and in the process of doing the details. I was supposed to trust his words and believe him when he said he was ready to fully be with me. Are we ever really ready to be vulnerable and open enough to expose the parts inside that so desperately want to remain hidden? These are the parts that we have hidden from ourselves, because we have not fully healed what we came here to touch and feel.

I began to feel creative and wrote this poem to express the feelings that were moving through me. I allowed myself to feel safe enough to let this part of me express to Steve my love and willingness to be in life with him.

The Dance

He walked into the room and I knew who he was.
His presence took my breath away and the dance began.
Each movement he made, every breath he took...
I felt it as if it were my own.
I witnessed someone I was meeting for the first time,
yet...I have known him for so long.
He lives in my heart.
I wanted to hear everything he had to say
as if no one else was in the room.
I know my past created walls around my heart,
for I was afraid to know this love again.
For the past has brought me pain....
maybe this time would be different.
As I remember now...
it is sweet pain that opens me to love again and again.
He danced with me that night
as his breath and skin touched me

in the most tender spot within my heart.
He held me safely with the confidence
that my heart remembered.
Without saying words,
he said, "I'm here, I'm showing up
to dance with you again."
My heart opened and I took his hand.
I melted into the place I knew
was the reunion of love known before.
Thank you for showing up to dance.

After three months of seeing him and not fully letting him into my life, I decided to believe his words and let myself fully love and be loved by this man. When I let the protection down I felt the love flow so beautifully. Life had taught me to move into the next step and to trust my heart. My heart said yes to the rest of the dance.

25

Life Seemed To Be Falling Apart

My landlord was waiting patiently for the rent I owed him. I was waiting for money to arrive from past work I had done with my sister in the cosmetic business. Changes in her company had created a number of problems. Finally a letter arrived – but it told me I would not be receiving any money at this time. I was, however, assured of a new position as a spokesperson with a contract and some sort of retainer. I waited patiently for this position to take form. Up to this point, my landlord had been understanding of my circumstances because he trusted me in his home. Then one day I received a phone call from Colleen. She told me that the company was closing and there would be no job.

Some weeks earlier, I had prayed, asking if I could support myself and my children comfortably just doing my spiritual work. It was truly what I wanted to focus my energy on, and my prayer was answered. That day, I went to the Unity Church knowing that it was important to go. At the service, the visiting reverend spoke of manifesting abundance. To give of time in love, we will receive time for ourselves. As we give money in the same easy manner, we receive the money.

I had twenty dollars. Nothing more in my wallet and nothing more in my bank account. Still, I felt the ease in giving to the church as if I had hundreds of dollars in my wallet. It was a feeling in me, the same feeling as when the energy of Divine love enters my being. So I gave with the fullness of my being.

At the end of the service a man approached me and asked me if I could do a session with him the next day. He was from India and I felt a beautiful heart connection in his presence. His name was Bo Najme. That night I had a dream in which he arrived at my house saying, "I found you, I found you." I asked him to lay on my massage table and I put my hands on him. He turned into a very old, wise man and then his physical body became his father.

The next day in preparation for my session with Bo Najme, I went into silence. I felt the importance of this meeting and felt I would likely share my dream with him. When he arrived, he was beaming love. I asked him to lie on the table and as I laid my hands on him, the presence of his father was in my conscious awareness as the light entered. His father had died at the young age that Bo was now and I began to speak the messages for him. His father was urging him to get in touch with his heart, or he would die young as he had.

The love was vast and when Bo opened his eyes he was filled with gratitude to have connected with Truth. He looked into my eyes and said, "Frannie, you were in my dream last night." I told him that he was also in mine. He began to share his dream by telling me a bit about himself.

"Did you know I am an inventor?" he asked. I did not know this. He continued saying, "In my dream I was inventing a way to get to you, to find you. I was in Chicago and I was driving on the highway – the Loop – and after going on it again and again, on the third trip, I found you." Well, with those words my heart expanded even more, as I remembered how he had entered my dream by saying, "I found you." He told me he had come to this country from India with fifteen dollars in his pocket and now he was a millionaire. "Frannie," he said, "the energy you share is like the energy of money." And then he wrote me a check for $100.

When he left, I knelt on the floor and wept, for I realized that through this man's voice I heard God say to me, "You are supported and abundant in My Love." The messenger came and I received the gift with gratitude. I took the money and bought groceries. When my children came home they were so excited, like it was Christmas. I felt the abundance so completely in my being and life – as if someone had given me a million dollars and this feeling continued to show me the truth.

Within days, many illusions shattered all at once. The contract with my sister's company had dissolved and I had two weeks to come up with $5,000. I could no longer afford the rent and realized I would have to move out of my house. My fears were challenging me and my faith was being tested. Maybe I could do this if there was only me, but I had Luke and Lane to care for. My emotional body began to overwhelm me. I called for help.

Over the phone, I shared my pain with Steve and as he held the space for me to share, I could feel him shift away. I was shattered. Was this really happening again… a man abandoning me when I was in my fear? This was my creation. In that moment I prayed he'd come to hold me.

When he did not, it validated the same old pattern that I was once again with a man who could not show up when I was in need. I understood that my neediness could push men away, yet I felt I was simply asking for support. I was not asking him to fix me, just to hold me. So I went to God, as I usually do, and there entered peace through my forgiveness.

My stuff had triggered his stuff – isn't that what we seem to do in relationship? The following weekend he finally arrived and one morning while we were wrapped in each other's arms, the love I felt touched my pain, my hurt, my fear and I opened up and shared.

To my shock and dismay, Steve began to share that he felt he couldn't be with me because he wanted a child of his own and did not think I could give him one.

It was like a knife in my heart as I allowed the roaring tears to flood out of my being. Was this true? I had thought that in my moment of great fear and darkness at least I had the security of Steve in my life. But as we know, there is no security but God's love, our own love. And in that moment I felt shattered – again.

As I look upon it now, I see how that day was a catalyst for my growth once again. Only God could shatter all my illusions to bring me into the flow of her Divine Plan. And as I moved into feeling the darkest shadows of my being, that plan began to unfold.

I awoke the next morning with no hope – in total doubt of why I was here. I was afraid. I was paralyzed with fear that the words I heard deep inside me were true – I could not make it, I could not support my children and myself doing my spiritual healing work.

So I embraced myself without judgment. I was with myself in a loving way, feeling and expressing where I was in that moment. My human ego was totally present as I cried for help, calling my sister-in-law Marion to speak to my heart. She knew what a challenge it was to be human and at that moment I trusted her to bring me truth. I went down to the beach with paper and pen, hoping some inspired words could bring me home to peace once again.

It was a calm day and the turquoise water of the Gulf brought me gently to my heart. I felt many feelings, overwhelming at times, as I breathed into the moment. I prayed so deeply to be free of the prison of my own ego. The outside world held me as if the arms of God were wrapping me up in a blanket of love.

Then, with a gentle beauty the peace entered and I felt the presence of Marion come into my space. In my mind's eye, I saw her sit with me, and the feeling to begin writing was very strong as the peace soothed me into the love and light of this energy. Words flowed so sweetly into my awareness. With ease and grace one word quickly followed the other, as I remained present in the nothingness beyond space and time.

The healing was magnificent as I re-read the words after the writing was complete. It felt as if the words were coming from beyond my own thinking and into my heart with no judgment. The presence unfolds and builds the energy of love as I surrender into the Knowingness of God. The guidance is received. It's all God because it's all love. These communications are my greatest teacher as my ego is revealed and the power of love fills my being.

I am now able to choose from love instead of fear. The letter from Marion touched me deeply:

So you ask for my help. I am here. I know you doubt everything today. I understand. So did I when I was in the physical world. There is a lot of truth to be learned by you today if you are willing to look and see the truth that is trying to come out of the circumstances. There is so much for you to understand about your soul's evolvement. There are lessons you are here to learn and these lessons appear through your conscious choice. You have free will and as you choose from this place and when I say this, it is for you to know that sometimes you are forced into decisions before you are ready to make them. So, when you sit with your self, feeling all of yourself, then the part of your life (the physical, your physical body) comes to you consciously. You can then begin to see when you are choosing your experience from the fullness of your own self worth. This experience – fully knowing your own self worth – will never be explained by anyone else but you. This is your journey and your experience is so personal that unless you go inside, you won't know who you are.

Listen to what I am saying. You have a great gift to go inside for another but it is most difficult for you to feel all of yourself. Right now there is so much going on in your mind and it is the part of you that wants to break away from these old patterns that keeps you so stuck and in a place of fear. The old pattern must be seen by you and you alone. I can help you because you have asked me to. That's the only way Spirit can help you. Did you know this? Well, you called for me and I heard you.

Frannie, I do not judge your ways in creating your life. I do not see anything but the love you want. It is what all mankind is searching for. I had the same struggles with my mind and my body as you did. There is so much denial in our minds it keeps our bodies so weak and vulnerable. First of all, you know that you have an inner knowingness in you that helps you to go inside your own heart when the outside world seems like it is betraying you. You cannot betray yourself. You can only go to your own desires and wants and know that this is okay. When you are fully honoring yourself, the world will support you. Understand what energy is – it all comes at you at once and if you don't know your self, your choice will not support your truth. You are so willing to give up your truth for love – you'll support another easier because you don't feel your own value. This is an issue for many. Yet when you really know yourself as you are beginning to understand, your own self will set you free.

"So Marion," I said. "What should I do now?"

Be patient with yourself – you are uncovering your so-called demons that keep you from creating the peace you so want. Relationships have uncovered a lot for you. Let Steve go right now. You can love him but love yourself more – give yourself the space to look at why things seem to be falling apart. You can only know yourself more. Go into the deep, dark places with enthusiasm and you will be so grateful. It isn't that you haven't done this before – you are going deeper. You are seeing why you lose yourself in another's dream. Remember Frannie – you have forgotten a lot of your own childhood for you attached yourself to another's life experiences – they seemed more real than your own. This life right now is your reality. You are here to be conscious of it and to uncover your true nature. The love is what is real and it is in you always. Feel this beautiful moment that we create together. I love this place and I remember it with you. The beach is a healing haven for lost souls. Your only responsibility is to discover your self.

Remember that laughter will help you see that sometimes life is one big joke after another. You can laugh at yourself with a full heart – isn't it funny how much pain we cause ourselves – now I am in Spirit and that pain was such a joke. Laugh at it, Frannie, until you feel the tears – cry until you feel the laughter – one big release for humanity...

Then I felt Jesus in my heart and my hand kept writing:

"*Sweet Beloved Child – your fear is not real. It is for you to continue to hold as if it were your child, as I hold you... without judgment. There is so much of your past wrapped into the moment of fear. You feel betrayed by me, yet it is you that has betrayed yourself for so long – and the guilt of your own separation seems to pull you into the place where you need validation through another that you are loved. This is your own process of self-discovery and I allow you to be there as long as you wish until the discomfort is unbearable to you. Then you reach for the Inner Light that holds you – it is I who holds you as you allow yourself to be held. Would it matter the experience that you have created? No, you have created it to uncover the part of you deep inside where you feel unworthy of Heaven. This seems like tedious work, yet most important to your own evolution and in turn the evolution of humanity.*

Your beloved Steve also awaits your return to Heaven as you await his. These are two human beings that have come together to know the truth. There is only one truth – you are love, you are loved and you are loving. Through this truth you come back to Heaven's gates as you embrace the part of you that believes the untruth. It is experienced in human relationship that the darkest part of the soul shows itself in the place where love is–for it will be set free. That is what a real relationship of heart is. Where each of you are willing to feel who you are in the moment of human experience to touch the truth of who you really are. There are no shortcuts – you are taking one step at a time as you feel yourself and you allow the moment to reveal the truth of the experience. There is no denying God's presence as you allow your denied deeper feelings to be held without judgment.

What does this mean? It is easier to hold the space for another when you feel yourself truthfully, not hiding, but being. The love is holding you in this safe place where Heaven can vibrate again. There is only one – look into yourself and see who you are in the eyes of humanity. There will be NO FEAR where love is allowed to be. Make room inside your heart as you let go of your own self-judgment."

So I looked at why my life seemed to be falling apart. I began to feel a freedom inside of me. I freed myself to allow Spirit to move through me again. I just needed to get out of the way, to let go of my own need to control, to make life happen. God knew my desire and that was all I needed to know. With this awareness, my heart opened fully again to the awesome experiences of my life. The miracle was the change in my mind. The shift happened as I received the truth the love revealed. I was in the flow again and I breathed in the sweet fullness of it. God's presence was more real in my life than ever.

I blessed the experiences that had brought me here. I now had the energy and enthusiasm to look for a new home. I had the energy and excitement to feel the partnership of God in my life. I had the energy and love to allow Steve to be who he was and to let him go on his journey with or without me. I was excited and I didn't know why. I wasn't feeling victimized. I felt empowered in my choices.

I continued to pack my house as I affirmed that the spiritual gifts would support my life in every way. I shared my story with my Tuesday meditation group in Sarasota. The power in the truth of where I was in surrender to God's plan was evident. I said to them, "God must have something awesome lined up for me, I might as well get out of the way."

The next night I received a message on my answering machine from Bo Najme, the beautiful man from India. "Frannie," he said, "I hope you don't mind that I know about your dilemma, but know that God is taking care of you." Then, this kind man gave me a gift of $6,000. He said, "Its just energy – the same energy you give." His generosity of money and spirit remind me of a profound passage from Paul Ferrini's book, *I am the Door*:

> "*Many beings of light have come as the Christ, bringing that simple reminder. All have the same purpose, for Christ is not a person, but a keeper of the flame, a giver of the gift, and a messenger of love. Light comes from him, because he has remembered light in the darkness of the world. Love comes from him, because he has received the gift and learned to give it unconditionally to all who would receive it.*"[17]

Bo Najme was definitely a messenger of God's love and an answer to my prayer. It was exactly what I needed to leave the house I was living in and start my new life.

Word got around that I needed a place to live with my two children. Just days before I had to leave the house on the Gulf, I received a call from my girlfriend, Lady Christopher Barrett, who lived in Boca Raton, Florida. She wondered if I would be interested in house-sitting her grandparents' Englewood estate until it was sold. I would need to be there while the real-estate agents showed it and I would have to make sure the gardener and the maintenance people showed up on time and did the needed work on this three-acre estate on the Bay.

When I went to see the house, I discovered a beautiful hexagon-shaped home on stilts. The sensation was like being in a birdhouse in the trees overlooking the land and the water. The energy was beautiful. I was once again in awe of God's plan. I could stay rent-free in this home until it sold. I could continue my Spiritual groups here. I was very excited as I thought of surprising my children with their new home. Even though I knew it was temporary, I saw the gift and I saw how God continued to take care of me.

Within a few days my friends helped me move and I was able to stay in this lovely place for six months. Unfortunately, (or as part of the divine plan) the house was sold a few days after Christmas – right in the middle of tourist season. I could not find a reasonable place to rent and ended up moving in with my parents. Luke and Lane chose to live with their father, who lived about twenty minutes away. I was torn, but as my son said, "Mom, it is time we lived with Dad; you go and do what you have to do for your life."

It was a very difficult time for me. Yes, I was grateful to have a place to live but I wanted to be with my children. It seemed God had a different plan for me. Just as Anandamayi Ma said in my dream, bliss was letting go of my attachments. Things weren't falling apart – I was ready to let go of more stuff.

I Love You Enough to Let You Go

I Love you enough to . . .
Allow you to find the God of your understanding
– however, whenever and if ever you choose.
Allow you to make what I perceive to be foolish mistakes.
Never possess you and never let you possess me.
Allow you to maintain your dignity
and never let you take away mine.
Allow you to seek help in your own way
– wherever and whenever you choose.
Leave your responsibilities in your hands

and to assume my own.
Allow you to hurt when you choose.
Never apologize nor cover up for you.
Be your best friend or never see you again.
Miss you but not be destroyed when we are out of touch.
Drop all of my expectations of you.
Become so serene and at peace that I don't 'need' you.
Let go of jealousy and anger.
Allow you to have your secret space and to have my own.
Listen to you with an open heart when I can.
Never tolerate your unacceptable behavior
– forgive your unacceptable behavior when and if I am ready.
Allow you to grow faster or slower than I do
without resentment.
Allow you to take magnificent care of yourself, your Spirit
and those things that are yours.
Allow you to become the beautiful person that you are.
I Love You Enough To Let You Go!

Author Anonymous

26

When You Know Your Work Works, It's Not Work

One day, before *A Course In Miracles* group I was facilitating, I was told that a group of people, including the minister of the local Methodist Church, would be joining us. I wasn't told the name, just "a minister." I didn't even know if it was a man or a woman. It made me feel very uncomfortable. To me, a minister was part of an organized religion and I was a spiritual woman bringing in messages from Spirit. I had my own picture of what this minister would look like and I felt the minister would have his or her own ideas about me.

Before the group arrived, I felt my fear. I was afraid of them coming, afraid I would be judged. I went inside myself and heard the voice say, *"Be all that you are."*

Then the minister showed up at the door – with her husband, Phil. As well as being a minister, she was also a beautiful young woman in her late twenties with long wavy hair down to her waist. Her name was Cheryl Smelser and she shattered any preconception I had, just by her appearance. Her radiant love joined instantly with my heart.

This meeting was the beginning of our friendship and our work together. Cheryl requested some private sessions with me. She was having a difficult time in her career as a minister, she explained. Since almost the very beginning of her ministry, her heart had been longing for a new path; yet it was difficult for her to even conceive of walking away. Her job was a good and secure one. She respected the church and the denomination, but felt she couldn't keep betraying her heart.

The emotional work Cheryl did through her sessions helped give her courage to eventually leave the Methodist Church. Her new career and life path began when she was hired to direct the volunteer program at Hospice. There, Cheryl felt fulfilled in her ministry. Her work with Hospice helped me too! She would call me when someone was in need of a spiritual counselor or just someone to lend an ear. My work with the dying taught me so much.

One day Cheryl called me from Hospice requesting my assistance. A man named Dick, who was in his mid-forties, was diagnosed with lung cancer and he was in his final stages before transition. Dick had read a book called *Talking To Heaven*, by James Van Praagh, which inspired him to ask many questions about what it would be like when his body dies and he leaves. He asked Cheryl if she knew anyone who could help him. Dick wanted to know what heaven was like. Cheryl thought of me immediately, so she called and asked if I would share my healing energy with him and allow Heaven's voice to move through me.

I arrived not knowing why God was connecting me with Dick, but honored to participate with Spirit. To bring peace and love to a dying man searching for understanding would also be a blessing for me. All I needed to do was to show up to be in service for God.

When I walked into his room at the Hospice house, I was shocked to see how old this forty-five-year-old man looked. He looked as if he was in his eighties. His body seemed so tired, aged and lifeless, from the pain of his disease. To be with him was easy for me and my non-attachment to him helped me let go of any personal thoughts of how I should be. Dick told me he was angry that he didn't get another chance in this life experience to be healthy. He was also embarrassed at his appearance and told me he had been a very good-looking man before the cancer took such a toll.

As I channeled Spirit, waves of love poured through me. Spirit had so much to share – to convince Dick that this was the best time of his life; that this illness was the perfect experience for him to know what was truly real. As I listened without judgment, I held back my own ego, fear and doubts, in order to give Spirit the space to speak.

In the light of Spirit, I didn't see him dying. I saw his Spiritual light and energy bright in the cells of his body, even as he questioned the experience that approached. I saw that he had many regrets and believed he had been cheated by God. In this space of non-attachment, I also witnessed the part of myself that had felt the same way at certain times in my life.

Because I had touched these angry feelings within myself around my own illness, I could hold the space for this man to feel. It is the part of ourselves which allows ego to be in charge, taking us away from the moment – the now – where everything exists. In this space we can witness our own dreams and desires, which have not manifested as we believed they should. In the moment of our disappointments, if we can trust, we are able to see the perfection of the events in our life. Now I can humbly bow to my life and how its unfolding has so perfectly brought me to who I am in this moment. I consciously choose to live in love, instead of pain and suffering. Love takes the complete focus of my heart. And in this place of love, it is easy to hold a space for another, as I can be that grace for myself.

Dick was angry at God for taking his life away from him. But it is our own responsibility to choose to live fully in the present moment. He thought he would never have another chance, but he was living his chance in that moment. If you understand cause and effect, you can be the cause and change the effect. No matter what the events of his life, of the illness he had created or the illness that was part of his destiny, he could change his life by changing his mind. He could change the whole meaning and experience of his life. It would not matter how many days he had left to live in a body. All that is important is this moment. If you are truly focused, the moment can be an eternity.

Why did God bring Dick and I together? He was definitely my teacher and a mirror for me as well.

I have learned that every experience is my teacher, if I just choose to be present with it. Sometimes we are not able to grasp a full understanding of our experience in the moment. But if we can embody the vibration, the energy will guide us and bring truth in the future. The moment can inspire you to change your old patterns of being and see your life with greater insight.

When I visited Dick, he would ask questions about what it would be like to be free from his body. He was very uncomfortable with his appearance in the last stages of his cancer. He often said he wished I had met him when he wasn't sick and dying. His eyes would light up like a child's when we talked about Spirit. He felt safe talking with me about his feelings regarding death and I appreciated his honesty. For some reason, the days I visited him always seemed to fall on Tuesday. We would talk about ourselves and it was very intimate.

One day we talked about him giving me a physical sign so I would know when he had crossed to the other side, moving beyond his physical body. He knocked on the wall seven times, KNOCK, KNOCK, KNOCK, KNOCK, KNOCK, KNOCK, KNOCK!!! That would be his sign.

I was excited to talk so freely of his transition. There was a part of me that wanted more proof of an afterlife, just as he did. We talked about his thoughts, about his fear of death. He felt heaven to be a place where he would be young again and free from his physical burdens. I liked his thoughts. He also thought he could come to me in Spirit, as my guide in some way. A guide that I had known in this life – I liked that idea too!

I enjoyed listening to his questioning mind. I heard his regrets and his anger about how he had chosen to live. I let him speak and I reminded him of the love that was ever present. Some days he was in so much pain we would just be in silence together. I would lay my hands on him, letting the energy move through me and speak to his inner heart. Then I would feel the energy of God move through my heart as I held the space for Dick to feel and hear whatever he needed.

Debbie in Spirit had done that for me. She showed me how the truth of the compassionate heart created the space for me and those I worked with. And my compassionate heart did become the space where Dick could feel his truth. As Debbie showed me how to die into Spirit, my essence was supporting Dick to know himself. The false self was the pain wanting to be heard. I know the pain and weakness and we can choose to listen to its truth.

One Tuesday morning I got a call from Dick saying he was too sick for me to come and visit. He thanked me for the gift I had shared with him. He told me he had experienced a lot of peace, but at the same time, it was bringing up a lot of fear for him. He felt he needed a break. It made me sad, because in my heart I knew I'd never see him again in the body. It was just a feeling.

But even this was a gift from Dick. It allowed me to acknowledge my own deep issues of abandonment. My friend didn't want me with him. And as I realized my disappointment, I let go and understood and was grateful for his honesty in the truth of who he was.

A week later I woke up early on a Monday morning and was inspired to write. These are the words that flowed effortlessly on the page:

"My beloved friend Dick is dying as I write. His body is dying and he is in and out of consciousness. I phoned Hospice and asked if someone would tell him that I loved him. I sit here in the silent light. I feel peace and I ask for the understanding and guidance of God at this time. I am filled with the light as it brings to me the communication from Jesus. As Jesus' presence is here with me, I feel him at Dick's bedside. God's light is touching my dear friend as it touches me. My mind and heart continue to say to Dick, "Go to the light, Dick. Go to the light." I am seeing the light for you, for we are one. You are in my heart, so we need not be in physical contact to be truly together. I share this love with you. I feel as if I'm sitting in your room at Hospice house, looking out the window at the orange trees, at the singing bird. It is angels who are singing to him through the bird's song.

I feel Dick's father, who is in the soul body at his bedside, guiding him to the light. I remember words from Elizabeth Kubler-Ross' book, *Death and Dying* – "*In the moments of sleep and unconsciousness before death, the dying are in a place where there is no time or space.*"[18]

Spirit loved ones who precede us in death, who loved us, are present and I know Dick can feel their presence. These beings, whether guardian angels, guides, or spirit loved ones, are helping him in the transition from life, to life after death.

Dick is shedding his cocoon and will be as free as a butterfly. He will have no pain, because he is no longer connected with the mind, his ego. He is soul – a Spirit Being who no longer needs a human experience.

I looked out of the window and so many butterflies began to fly around the deck and garden outside the window of my room. My heart expanded as I felt the joy of those beautiful creations of God.

And then, the sign came. Seven knocks on the wall, KNOCK, KNOCK, KNOCK, KNOCK, KNOCK, KNOCK, KNOCK, just as Dick had promised! I felt Dick's energy enter my heart and the feeling was so beautiful as I felt the joy of his transition into the light. I felt our energies merge as we traveled together into a vast field. In this vision I saw in my mind's eye, we were young adults running through the grass, laughing. As we fell to the earth, I saw Dick laughing, happy and free. The joy radiated from his presence. He was free and I was filled with a wondrous peace.

Perhaps Dick had not fully left his body yet, but was already beginning to experience the freedom of his Spirit. I felt in my heart he was unconscious, yet ready to depart this world. I called Hospice and a nurse confirmed that Dick was unconscious and assured me that someone had whispered in his ear, "'I love you,' from Frannie."

Conscious connection is the awareness of the moment when the Holy Spirit enters your being in the power of Love. The energy is felt deep inside the heart where the stillness of mind begins to birth the knowledge of all creation.

The next day I awoke feeling uncomfortable. I felt distracted by the outer world. I tried to write, but nothing seemed to flow. I felt as if I was creating experiences to busy my mind, as if I chose not to feel my heart. As I sat with myself, I witnessed this experience.

I believed I was blocked, but why?

That night I sat thinking about my frustrating day, asking why was I feeling depressed. By this time I had already facilitated a group meditation, which brought much love and light into my being, so I was open and in the flow, again.

The realization finally came to me – Dick had died and the block was my grief. I was not allowing myself to be fully conscious of the fact that my friend had died.

When we are blocked, we cannot feel Spirit and my unacknowledged, subconscious feelings of grief were blocking the truth of his death, which I did not consciously want to hear.

The next morning while driving, I turned on the radio. The song playing spoke directly to my heart – "The Freedom of the Butterfly." My heart opened and I heard a voice from Spirit, "I am free now." I knew it was Dick. I knew he had died yesterday and was now Living Spirit. Joy moved through me.

When I arrived home the phone rang. Even before I picked it up, I knew it was my friend Cheryl from Hospice calling to tell me that Dick had made his transition. The day before I had tried calling Hospice three times, but no one had answered. I now believed I was supposed to have this experience, to validate the communication of Spirit, to know that we will always receive the truth in God's time.

Dick is free. I celebrate his living Spirit as he continues to live on in my heart.

What is heaven like? My mind is so full of questions. *Can you hear me, Dick? What is it like to be free of body and mind? Were you afraid when you knew it was time to leave? Did you know when it was time to go to the light?*

Dick - is it like you thought and can you do whatever your heart wants? Are all your questions answered? Who is with you? Do you know why we met at the end of your life in this body? You knocked on my wall and I felt you go into the worlds of God from which you came. I felt you as if you were walking into my room; I was filled with energy and there were no questions when I felt you.

I knew God in that moment.

I felt the vastness of Spirit.

I remembered that we were one.

I am so grateful to have met you.

I know you can hear me.

I heard the birds singing in the bright sunlight outside my window. There was so much happening outside. The song of the birds got louder as I brought my awareness there - outside of me I saw without my physical eyes. I saw the calmness of the day and yet the wind blew through the trees making its presence known to me. I received and acknowledged the gift of nature as it supported me. I sat patiently for the entry of the words from Spirit. There was so much peace in my being. That was the reason for me to be here, to witness the peace of God's presence in my moment. My pen wrote the words that are the vibration of this peace that human beings are in search of. As it embraces me, I share it with all:

"Precious child of God, you are my partner in Light to dance with the world. Your ability to choose your state of being is the experience of All through Our Presence. I am walking with you as you choose this Love of Heart. I am touching humanity as you touch the light for yourself. I am with you wherever you go. I am with you in the silence when you think you are alone. The light is moving through you when you read these words. It is I who speak to your heart, calling you to join in the journey home. Home is the place within, where embodiment of Spirit shows you the way to your homecoming. I am the hands which lift you out of darkness, when you

experience heaviness of heart and you cannot see where you are going. The light may be dim for you, but My love for you will never let you down. As you surrender to My Presence, the inward journey guides you back to the Kingdom where God awaits you, for you are His treasure. You are His precious child coming back to the arms of love. This is the experience of peace that will become the open heart for your brothers and sisters. The remembrance of being home will be the love shared. There is the purpose of living in this body. The purpose comes to you because you are ready to serve from this place of peace if you have found it within your own heart. You hold the treasure that God has created for you and this treasure you share with the world. It is the Holy Spirit's touch in every moment of conscious awareness.

This experience enters because you are willing to be in the moment in a way different from the ego's experience. You are willing to be the one that knows God is here with you now and I am the One that will remind you, my dear friend.

As you sit here in peace with the moment, your light radiates far beyond this world. It touches every part of creation. As you focus, the energy moves into that place where your intention is. In your state of heart, you are with your friend Dick. As your hand, as by My hand, we lead our brother into freedom.

He is not alone. He welcomes your love, and the peace he feels now is what he did experience in your physical presence. He remembers, because you remember. This man who is leaving this human experience will live on in the hearts of everyone and everything he consciously touched in his life. Conscious awareness is the key as you allow the energy to continue to be alive in all things. Every connection will inspire thoughts to create an opening for his Spirit to enter this world you are part of. Spirit living on and on through the hearts of the ones left behind. Wherever he did walk, nature embraces the part of him that will continue to be a part of creation for all eternity.

Any thought you have of Dick is the continuation of his Spirit living on to love the world, to heal the world. Understanding the beauty of death frees the Spirit to live beyond the illusions created by humanity's belief in separation. There is no fear in his being – for in Spirit there is no ego. The precious child has come home into the wholeness of his being to remind all that we are home again in our own hearts."

When we are able to go inside and hear our own self, we can then be the compassionate heart hearing another, no matter what they need to say. The compassion that comes through is definitely rooted in the acceptance of who we are. When we are living someone else's life, or when we are living a life that others want us to live, we cannot develop the acceptance of who we are. When we accept ourselves, get comfortable with who and what we are, then when someone else presents to us what is their authenticity, we can support it. We can recognize when they are having trouble accepting who they are.

When people are real and for me that means sharing their darkness and fear as well as the love, I can really connect. I have compassion because I know what it is like, because I have embraced my own darkness and fear. I don't have to fix them, just love them with compassion.

When someone is in pain and they present their fear to us, we think we have to fix them. It is the same dynamic – different sides of the same coin. When we think we want to fix someone else it is because they trigger some insecurity in ourselves, which we feel we must fix. The need to fix others' lives comes from wanting to fix ourselves because we believe something is wrong with us. When we feel we are missing something, then we try to get something to fill ourselves. Often we feel we can do this by 'fixing' others, thereby earning their gratitude and love.

We feel the only way we can ever be really helpful to anyone else is by healing the essence of the person who is being compromised by their fear. In truth, we cannot heal them, but we can hear them. By hearing them we are reaffirming the essence of their person, reaffirming that they are not the victim and are capable of doing whatever they need to do. They are capable of making the connection to love.

By being the presence of love for them, we can help them to tune into the presence of love within themselves. But we do not attach ourselves, or give energy to their fears. We only allow the space for the person to confront their own fears. We are saying "I support you in being fully who you are," whatever that means. That is my work. That is why it works, because I hold the space of unconditional love.

When you know your work works, it is not work. How can you hear another person, unless you have heard yourself?

When someone comes in fear, you will react to their fear if you haven't established who you are. In that way the person is triggering you. We can only be helpful to someone if we don't buy into their fear. We must work with our own fear. That's why the reflection of relationship is so wonderful. In knowing myself I can be a loving heart for the living and the dying.

My relationship with Cheryl has brought me many gifts. I have learned so much from the experiences I have shared with people, like Dick, who are transitioning to life after death. And through my work with Cheryl, I learned that as in death, Spirit also transitions into life on earth. Birth.

Cheryl and her husband decided it was time to have a child. In our sessions following that decision, Cheryl and I felt the presence of two souls. While it was common for us to feel the presence of many spirit loved ones during our sessions, this energy was different. Full of love, joy and happiness, these souls conveyed to us they were awaiting transition to be born.

I encouraged Cheryl to have a relationship with these souls now and be open to communication through dreams and meditation. During one of our sessions, we felt one soul's bubbly, giggling personality, and Cheryl began laughing uncontrollably. We asked for the name and I heard Asarah! Then the energy told Cheryl she could call her Sarah. We also felt the energy of another, a boy. One day Cheryl called to tell me she had heard the name Daniel and had seen him in her dream so clearly while holding him as a baby in the bathtub. Within two and a half years, Cheryl and her husband had two children – Sarah came first, followed by Daniel. I am blessed to have them in my life as my Godchildren.

27

There Are No Mistakes

I was called, again, to go to the Hospice House, to be with a terminally ill patient named Cheryl Jensen. She knew she was dying. The doctors had told her that there was nothing more they could do for her. She had gone through so much to keep her body alive. In 1987 she was diagnosed with breast cancer, followed by liver cancer, a bone marrow transplant and then Christmas 1998, a brain tumor and probably much, much more. She had been a caregiver her whole life.

I was told she just wanted to meet someone who would understand all the spiritual experiences she was having. I could be her spiritual friend, someone who was not caught up in her personal life.

The day I walked into her room at Hospice House I felt a kindred spirit with her. I felt comfortable as she asked me to sit down on the sofa with her. She began to talk quickly, sharing a lot of information about herself and her illness. I listened very intently because I was amazed to hear of all her health challenges. Her body looked so weak, yet I felt great strength in her Spirit. Because of chemotherapy, she had no hair and her skin was pasty white. She looked tired but excited to share with me her experiences. Maybe she felt I would not judge her and hoped I would understand her process.

I related so much to her because of my own illness. It was in 1987 when I had first become ill and my own life became focused on my journey to heal this body. Here she was in a very weak, sick body and I was healthier than ever in mine. Cheryl had chosen to use allopathic medicine and I had chosen alternative medicine. I did not use any medicine but herbs and Cheryl had chosen to use the chemicals. She had been a nurse and that was what she knew.

Yet sitting with her, I felt that her Spirit was so wise and so huge. I listened to her every word because I felt she was a teacher for me right now, someone to show me conscious living in her dying. I felt honored that God brought us together.

I chose not to share my personal story because I wanted to be the listener and I wanted to hold the space for Cheryl in whatever way she needed me to. Cheryl told me that a voice had spoken to her just two weeks before she was diagnosed with a brain tumor. At the time, she was on a spiritual high and felt blessed to have had the experience. The voice had said, "Cheryl, there is only one more thing you have to experience in this life. It is to experience your dying. Remember that you can make no mistakes and the purpose was to love yourself." Cheryl told me it was a relief to find out that she was now going to die. She said that when she accepted her death, there was no more fear.

I asked Cheryl if she would like to come to one of my meditation groups and she was very happy to go with me. I loved being with her because she was like a child who could only tell the truth of what was going on in that very moment. If she didn't like what I said, she would say so. There was no holding back on my account. Sometimes I wanted to laugh and sometimes I felt so frustrated with her. I was with someone who really was not attached to being liked. She was just being herself. Because these days were so precious for her, she would get directly to the point and always tell the truth. She did not hide the fact that she was dying.

The group sat with her in an honoring way. Many of them had never been with someone so close to transition. She talked about her experiences and told me later she sometimes couldn't tell the difference between this world and the non-physical world. She was aware of her light body communicating with the people in the group. She even thought she had walked over to one of the women and given her a gift. She didn't know if she had done it in the physical or not. I assured her it was in her light body because I had not seen her physically get up at all.

The next week when I arrived to get her, she was all dressed up, even wearing a wig. The Hospice nurses were quite excited with her progress, saying she had a lot more energy and was happier. I enjoyed her company and all that she shared with me and with the group. It was a different kind of a friendship for me. I knew we did not have to get into our personal history because the gift was in the moment. We were sharing who we were right now.

In some ways it was difficult to stay that present, knowing her death was near. Each time I was with her, I wondered if I would see her again and that made the moment even more special. I realized this was the way I wanted to be in all of my relationships – to savor each precious moment and not take it for granted that I would see them again.

I called Cheryl one morning to see if I could take her out to dinner before attending the meditation group. She sounded confused and disoriented, but said she would like it very much. When I arrived at her room that evening, it was dark, so I peeked around the corner to see if I could find her. She was sitting on a chair in the shower. Her body was skin and bones, pure white, with no hair. At a distance you would not know if she was a man or a woman. She was surprised that it was 5:30 p.m., but I said not to worry.

I tried to help her, but she was very independent. She began to put toothpaste on her legs, instead of moisturizer cream. She wanted to be alone, so I returned to the lobby and prayed. She was in no state to go anywhere. When I returned to her room, she had her pajamas on and said she had already eaten while I was in the lobby. I knew she had not. I went out to get her some food but she couldn't eat it. I felt she was in her last days.

I had to leave her, but brought her to the meditation group in my heart. As a group, we prayed for Cheryl that night and it touched us all deeply. All we could do was love her where she was in that moment.

Early in the morning, two days later, I heard Cheryl's voice in my head. I called her right away and Ellie, her nurse, answered the phone. She told me Cheryl was in a bad state and couldn't speak at all. I drove right there. I asked for peace in my heart and I could feel it in me. As I stood before her, she opened her eyes and smiled. I felt she recognized me as I touched her and loved her. I said my good-byes telepathically and could feel her already beyond her body. The tears rolled down my face and enormous gratitude filled my body and heart with so much love. She fell asleep and I left knowing I would not see her alive in this body again.

A few days later on a Sunday morning, I woke out of a deep sleep feeling great grief in my body. I thought I was missing my children and I cried in Steve's arms. I heard the phone ring. Cheryl had died at 7 a.m. that morning. I then felt the joy that she was now free in Spirit.

Cheryl gave me a beautiful gift – a reflection of non-attachment. This experience of letting go of attachments sets you free to be with yourself; to experience every moment in acceptance without fixing or abandoning. This is truly freedom.

I didn't know Cheryl very long but our friendship in her last days changed my life. She was real, authentic and pure love. As I watched, she let go of all her attachments – her home, her car, her work, even her family. She said good-bye to life in her body and was fully present in her dying. Then she slipped from the body into the truth of who she was – the true nature of Spirit, which is in everything.

A few days after her passing, I awoke early. As I meditated, I moved deeply into a very clear state. Cheryl entered the room appearing, like a Buddhist monk, and sat cross-legged on the bed beside me. At first I was afraid. When I realized there was no need for fear, I opened myself to the experience as energy filled the room and me. There was a deep knowingness and silence within her. Without speaking to one another, I heard her and felt her. After a long time of silence, I asked her... "What is heaven like?" Without moving to look at me she answered, "This is heaven."

I could feel heaven in me as the experience of being. She was watching a big screen as if she was witnessing life in a non-attached way. Then I felt I was holding a baby in my arms. As it nestled against my chest, I knew this baby was me. I awoke from this blissful state and saw that two hours had passed since I had begun to meditate. I picked up a pen and wrote these words.

I felt they were the energy of Cheryl.

"You have healed your body through self-love. Your heart knows the truth of which you are. Your intention from the onset of your illness was to bring love into your own self. Your life became a reflection of that intention. When illness comes to an individual, it is a wake-up call. When tragedy comes to mankind, it is a wake-up call, to bring pure conscious awareness to the experience of living in this body, in this world. There is so much for you to tap into. There is so much love to be brought into this world through your own individual heart, as human beings. Or might I say, being a human.

Now that I have let go of the material world and I have become my true nature, I have become more a part of you and all creation. We are one in heart and energy. This experience is what you bring to this human world. The experience of pure, conscious being. And its expression in form is love.

Be at peace knowing that your commitment to self-love has brought more love to every part of your life and so it is that the world is healed in your presence. You are able to be the reflection of this Divine love for all that join you in any moment. Moment-by-moment let life unfold for you as it has been planned. Let go of the preconceived ideas that you have anything to do with creation but to be creating this moment of love."

Remember there are no mistakes... Cheryl showed me how to let go of the attachments of this world to be the presence of heaven in a body.

28

The Touch Of A Master

My life was changing again. Lane and Luke's father had married an American woman, Nancy, and they were all in the process of getting their legal documents to live in the United States. Now that the children were taken care of, I had to take care of myself. I did not have a green card and I could not legally remain in the U.S.A. any longer. Steve and I were seeing one another again but he had made it clear he did not want a committed relationship, so marriage was out of the question. I would have married him in a heartbeat but it was not the time for him. He was not ready and I did my best to accept his decision.

I moved into my parents' home and began making plans to move back to Canada. It was time for me to realize my own dream again. I focused my energy on writing my book and doing my sessions with clients and meditation circles. It wasn't easy for me to be without Luke and Lane but I was grateful I had a few months to live near them while I was with my parents. It made letting go a more gradual process as I was able to see them every week.

Enormous sadness would overtake me sometimes and I would just fall to the floor as my weakened legs gave way. The grief of not having my children living with me was almost too much for my heart to bear. But, I also saw the wonderful opportunities to be with my mom and dad again, to enjoy them and share in their lives.

Each morning, I got up early to write and my dad often joined me. He would knock on my door and ask to hear what I had written the night before. He loved my intimate sharing. Sometimes he would cry as we touched the memories and feelings of our past together. He now gave me the attention he could not give me as a child, when he was busy with work and his own problems of survival.

I loved our time together. He encouraged me – saying he did not usually like women authors, but that he really enjoyed my writing. My mom cooked for me which helped me focus on what I wanted to accomplish.

They both held me in their arms when I cried the tears of my hurt and pain. Lane was thirteen years old and Luke was sixteen. I now see how this divine set-up enabled me to go inside, take care of the things, and let go. I had put so much on the back burner when the kids were living with me. There were a lot of feelings I needed to resolve. Writing this book was important for me. Writing helped me to heal.

Still, I felt devastated by my situation. I did not want to move back to Canada. I did not want to leave my children and my life in Florida. I was heart broken that Steve chose not to commit to me. Luke and Lane were living with their father and Nancy now. And even though my mind said, "This is part of the plan," I was just not ready to let go of them. Deep down, I believed that the souls of my children were supposed to be with Nancy, their stepmother. Maybe there was something she could bring to Luke and Lane that was important for their growth and maybe there was something Luke and Lane could share with her.

Luke had his driver's license now, so after I had said goodbye to all of my friends, he and Lane took me to the airport. At the gate, Lane's arms were around me and Luke held my hand as we sat. I blurted out those things moms say, like, "Call me anytime you need me." "Be present whenever you are driving, Luke!" and "You are the best children a mom could ever have!" My heart broke as tears ran down my cheeks but I tried to be strong. I held it in, knowing that I had to or it would be harder for them.

Inside, I think I was still waiting for a miracle. Maybe Steve would run through the airport terminal, like in the movies, yelling, "Stay! Stay! Marry me! I can't live without you!" But of course, that did not happen.

Lane   *Frannie*   *Luke*

Luke, who had been staring off and thinking deeply, suddenly said from his heart, "Mom, you see that guy walking there? He's going to sit beside you on the plane…"

"Oh Luke, please," I protested, "I'm not interested in another man, especially right now."

They called for boarding but I wanted to stay with my kids until the last minute. I was the last person to board the airplane. Holding back my tears, I looked for my seat.

And there he was, the guy Luke pointed out to me. I should have known that Luke was telling me the future. My seat was at the window, his was on the aisle and there was an empty seat between us, thank goodness. I didn't want to make eye contact because I didn't want to talk. I just wanted to curl up in my corner and be with my grief.

So that is what I did. I cried and cried and cried, uncontrollably. I couldn't stop. It didn't matter where I was. I was in my deep, deep sadness. I cried because I knew that my life was changing and I was surrendering to it.

I covered myself up with the blanket and fell asleep. When I woke up, I heard the pilot saying we couldn't land because of a line-up on the runway. He said we would have to circle for a while.

I had a connecting flight and not much leeway with time. I began to meditate and I could hear my inner voice urging me to connect with the man Luke had pointed out. But I ignored the urge. I continued to stay inside myself until the pilot came on again and said, "We will have to circle for a while longer." The voice inside added, "*Until you connect with this person, we will continue to circle and you will miss your connecting flight!*"

"All right," I said inside. I had heard and this time I listened. I turned to the man in the other seat and said, "Hi. I have to connect with you or we won't land." He laughed and said, "I know. I'm a martial arts teacher and I know about energy. I was feeling that you needed space so I held the energy for you."

We talked and it was pleasant. Then I asked him his name. "Steve," he replied.

The moment I connected with him, we began our descent and landed. I felt God's presence embracing me while he held a space for me. Maybe this Steve was a messenger from the higher self of my Steve, who couldn't be there for me in the physical. This man carried my bags as we ran to catch my connecting flight. He definitely was an angel in my life that day.

Leaving my children, the man I loved, my friends, the Gulf of Mexico and the life I had created for twelve years was really happening. My gut and my heart ached so much with grief it felt like someone had died. I guess the life I had *was* dying, as I left the United States to start my new life back in Ontario, Canada where I was born.

Before I went back to Canada, I took a little side trip to California to spend some time with my dear friends Kristine and Jacques. It was the perfect place for me to be with all my feelings. As I rested, I discovered much wisdom in the words of author Wayne Muller whose book, *Sabbath: Finding Rest, Renewal, and Delight*

In Our Busy Lives, provided me with the insights and change in attitude I needed to walk into the new life that lay ahead for me in Ontario. I took to heart his advocacy for Sabbath... "Like a path through the forest, Sabbath creates a marker for ourselves so, if we are lost, we can find our way back to our center. 'Remember the Sabbath' means 'Remember that everything you have received is a blessing. Remember to delight in your life, in the fruits of your labor. Remember to stop and offer thanks for the wonder of it.' *Remember*, as if we would forget."[19]

Our friendship helped lift my spirits and give me time to rest and remember. As we walked through the airport after a nurturing week with Kristine, I felt ready for the new adventure, or as ready as I could be with an open heart and mind.

At one of the gates, we noticed quite a few natives of India congregated around a sign welcoming a beloved brother to the United States. I was drawn to this crowd of people. Somewhere deep inside I felt I needed to meet this person, or at least just witness him. I said to Kristine, "I think he is a Master." In that moment he stepped through the gate into a procession of people bowing and giving him gifts of flowers. He was a small, humble man; yet his energy was huge and so radiant. A current of energy moved through my body in a way I'd never experienced before. Kristine felt it, too. We were witnessing a living master. As Kristine and I watched this event, both of us were enveloped with truth chills running up and down our spine, as every cell of our being received the blessings of his presence. This energy did not stop moving in us while in his presence.

I walked towards the crowd gathered around him as if something was pulling me. "Who is he?" I asked a man taking pictures. "He is the master of the Sindhi religion," he replied. I saw his devotees bow down and touch his feet or kiss his hand. I looked at him and his eyes met mine. The love was radiating into my heart and I heard him speak to me inwardly, "Come, you are welcome too!"

I felt like a child going to sit on Santa Claus' knee as I hurried through the crowd. I looked into his welcoming eyes as I touched his hands. His light seemed to get brighter and all I could feel was total love and energy running up and down my spine. I felt pure joy and happiness as he handed me the same gift he was giving everyone, wrapped in a red paper. It made me grin when I looked down and saw that it was a Kit Kat chocolate bar.

The joy and happiness that was radiating in him was now in us. It was a blessing and a healing. This man was the embodiment of love, the master of love. I had just been reading a book by Miguel Ruiz called *The Mastery Of Love*. We can all be this love. This beautiful man was my reflection.

As I said good-bye to my dear friend Kristine, I could feel the love in both of us. I could feel the healing I had received by being in the presence of a master who was grounded in his body and filled with Spirit. I could feel my grounding deep down through my legs and into the earth.

I felt that it was now time for me to ground this energy of Spirit into my life through my body. I could be the truth of who I am as I let go of the fears and the dramas of my past. I could touch Canada just as this humble man of radiant light touched America. He left his home of India to touch us. He modeled for me the living Spirit in a body, like many masters who have walked the earth. I can be the model of God's radiant love as I walk upon this earth being the presence of Spirit in my body. It only takes one of us to remember.

A few months later, I went back to Florida to visit Lane. Fate took me back to my Steve again, maybe just for some closure. A dream moved me to go and see him. Standing in his house, he looked at me. "How could you come?" he asked. " I have been so mean." I just looked at him, knowing it was always just his fear.

"I believe in the love, I believe in you," I replied. Maybe I just wanted to show him that through it all, I still loved him. Maybe I wanted to set us both free. It wasn't that his behavior hadn't hurt me. Still, I knew his behavior reflected what he believed at the time because of his past hurts and pain.

I returned to Canada holding a space for Steve, but releasing my attachment to "us." I always believed that when I wasn't in my own patterns of self-betrayal and fear, I could be with him and not betray myself.

I had healed. I know now that I can hold a space in my heart, even when someone is in their fearful shadow behaviors. I can still believe in who they are, just as they are.

29

Sam And The Geese

I had just returned to Canada and was up at my parents' summer home in Northern Ontario. It had been our family cottage and I loved it there. It was late one evening when I received a call from a woman named Dawn Johnson. Dawn wanted my help in connecting with her six-year-old son Sam, who had passed away in April. At that time, I also had been contacted by three other mothers, all who had sons who died around the same day as Sam. When Dawn called, I made an appointment for the next morning with her and her husband, Tim.

The Johnsons had been referred by a mutual friend, Janet. She told them about the work I do and that I might possibly help them with their pain and their many questions about where and how Sam was. Janet was a long-time friend of mine. She had been a stylist for one of the studios where I'd spent a lot of time working when I was a full-time model. We were like family there and Janet was one of the people who always seemed to be interested in who I was, not just what I looked like. Her job was to make the clothes look great on the model by pinning, stuffing and cutting. Yet behind the storefront of her job, Janet was also connecting in deeper, more personal ways.

Years after my departure from the modeling business, I got a call from Janet. She had tracked me down in Florida at my home on the Gulf of Mexico and was interested in the work I was doing with my Spiritual gifts. Janet had been struggling with chronic fatigue for some years and knowing how sick I had been, wanted to know how I had healed myself. So she came to a Goddess weekend in Florida and we reconnected in a wonderful way. Even though her path to spirit was different from mine, we were in the same place and maintained the contact.

A couple of years later, Janet called to tell me her mother had passed away. We scheduled a session to see if I could connect with her mom. When Janet called for her appointment, I saw her mom, in Spirit. She sat on my bed, in a peachy-coral dress, holding her little dog on her lap. She shared truth and love for her daughter. The communication touched Janet deeply, and helped her heal the pain she felt around her mother's death. That is why Janet felt confident I could help her friends, Dawn and Tim.

I did not know any of the details surrounding Sam's death, but I went to sleep that night praying I could be a vessel for the truth that could help these people in their terrible grief. I had a pen and paper by my bed in case I received a dream or some messages through the night. If I don't write it down right away, I sometimes forget because it feels like a dream. I woke up around two a.m. What I saw was a goose or a duck. In that dream state it is my own interpretation. I wrote down all the information I could remember. It didn't matter if it made sense to me or not, I was just the channel for this connection. Then it was like watching a movie. I saw an adult man walking, and then a man's right arm trying to grab a child's hand. Then the child disappeared. I woke up with a lot of tightness in my chest. I felt despair, pain and fear.

I meditated for about an hour to clear and then connected with Dawn. These are the words I wrote:

"So much began to come to me. I could not retain it so I allowed myself to be the energy – trusting all would be revealed at the right time. Getting familiar with the energy of the Johnsons... purple light... Jesus came holding Sam. I heard... "I'm okay, I'm okay... looking for Grampa or Granpapa." He sat on the bed like a child would, on his knees, gentle yet restless, resting his head on his hands, laying on his stomach looking up at me. There was strong purple light as I feel myself connecting with Dawn. She's sleeping and Sam is visiting her and he enters her dream state. Will she remember? I hold the space for her to remember. I see Sam again as if he is looking through the bedroom window. His hands are cupped around the glass to see in, he is here in my presence. He chose me to get to his family. I thank him."

When Dawn and Tim called I was able to tell them what I received. Not knowing how Sam died I wondered how this information would help them. As I shared my experience they seemed quite emotional in their silence and told me they would call me back.

When they called back, they told me that Sam fell through the ice of the pond beside the icebound floating dock on their country property and died. He and his sisters had been warned the day before not to go on the pond – that the ice was no longer safe. On the day he died, Tim and Dawn were away for the weekend and had left their children with a nanny.

They told me that Sam had two Grandfathers who were in Spirit. He was saying he was okay and with them both. They also told me that a man with a dog had seen Sam and had gone out to the dock and risked his life trying to reach him. They felt that Sam was showing me what he had seen at the end of his life on earth, from his position in the water. I was filled with emotion myself. I knew in every cell of my being that Sam was making this connection with us for a very important reason.

When I got off the phone I went out to the dock where my parents and Colleen were sitting. They had gone outside so it would be quiet in the house while I spoke with Dawn and Tim. My family told me that the whole time I was on the phone there were five Canada geese at the end of the dock. They had never witnessed Canada geese at this time of the summer. They are usually on the lake in late fall and this was the end of July.

The next morning Sam came into my inner space and spoke to me for what seemed to be a very long time. It was like talking to a friend. I could hear Canada geese honking as I was in purple light and feeling the gentle energy of his presence. Sam took me in my visions to the dock on the pond near his home and I felt I was a part of the energy of it all. Then I felt I was experiencing this through Dawn's expression.

I could feel the difference between Sam's experience and Dawn's experience. He kept speaking gently as I asked questions.

I wanted to write but he said it was important for me to experience this communication. Then my sister Colleen came into the room and I spoke from this expanded state and asked her to listen to the words as she turned on the tape recorder. Sam's energy moved with mine. I felt a oneness so that I could bring through the thoughts and information. When the communication ended, the Canada geese flew away honking as I felt Sam's energy leave, or perhaps I should say, I left Sam's energy. I knew why I had come to the lake house now – it was to witness the Canada geese and how Sam used them to form his energy and bring communication to our hearts.

Now I will share the words that I transcribed from the tape. Not all the words were clear so there are dots where I could not hear clearly. I felt Sam's energy to be much vaster than that of a six-year-old boy. I felt he was an old soul as I heard telepathically that he was Samuel:

"...children only learn to be attached to the past through the example of the living, but it is all part of soul's evolution...all of this energy can be formed by each person, just as the energy of Samuel as the Canada goose." (*I was speaking what I was receiving into the tape recorder*). Samuel took me into his home, the dock, the land of his birth. I have no attachment to it.

"This is a lifelong journey, for the soul is experiencing in body. (These thoughts that are moving through me... Samuel is bringing them to me.) So intricate is this design. When we are present in every moment, it becomes so vast and eternal. That which we are supposed to remember or will choose to remember is energy to be brought forth in the next moment. It is a part of your world's intricate design. It is the experience that is here now. And when a human being remembers this experience of being, the moment of creation, it is formed." Samuel came to me in the dream, connecting to me and, in a more conscious way, to his family. He wanted to share himself as he now was as spirit – a higher purpose, memory, symbols, views, a bridge from the unseen world to this physical world, a connection between Spirit and physical realities.

"When there is attachment to a thought form created from fear, it would mean that the soul would be part of the darkened thought of fear, not the illuminated thought of love. Attachments, thought forms that keep one stagnant from the thought of the presence, will create this experience as the opening. The experience of letting go is where the opening is for Spirit to move into this dimension. This is the grieving process as well as the letting go process of attachments.

The dimensions beyond this one rest gently between the hearts of humanity. Not a place to go to to be rid of this world of pain and suffering, but the place within every heart that chooses all that God is. It is all energy being formed. It is all the same. It is how one perceives it and how one forms it. Let it be in the moment moving into formlessness through one's heart.

If one could experience the birth of this energy, to be the infinite form of God, that same energy is what leaves the body at death. Its intelligence cannot be understood by a human mind, only the heart that is free to Love as God is. When one can let go of the form, the experience of God is and is in all things."

With the tape still rolling, I describe to Colleen these thoughts:

"As this information as energy moves through me, it is the same energy, Samuel. It is how one perceives and lives it. Because I have no attachment to Samuel as Sam, I can hear him as its energy moves through my own thought creating a space within my own presence in a form as energy touching the world.

This is where we are all one. This is where we are no different than anything in creation. This energy that we are can move into the birds, the trees, into the earth, the children, into our presence. We are born of this world for our own soul's evolution. I feel the presence of many..."

When I shared this information with Dawn and Tim, I understood their resistance to it. They longed to feel Sam as their six-year-old little boy, not this vast energy of Samuel.

The next morning I woke up at 6:20 a.m. and I felt Sam's presence as he spoke to my heart asking me to come outside and sit on the dock. He had something to show me. I walked onto the dock and as I sat at the end looking out onto the water, I kept seeing a vision of a dog in my minds eye. The dog was black and white. Then nature seemed to wake up. The cows somewhere far away all started mooing together, birds flying low in front of me, geese honking, fish jumping, crickets chirping, all at once like an orchestra. Then I heard the music of "Old MacDonald Had A Farm." I opened my eyes and saw everything illuminated. Then these words came as I wrote...

Dear Mom and Dad,

This is a letter to you as I am still connected so to your life. Your thoughts and prayers help me because it is an energy. As human beings we are living on the earth fulfilling only part of the whole that exists. When you are conscious of other dimensional selves, then you can expand your awareness.

As a six-year-old boy I lived the part of me that could remember soul. Now as Spirit, I am living energy able to connect with presence to all other dimensions.

As you, my soul continues to evolve the same as all, yet now there is no fear. This does not exist as energy in a place as I am. There are schools here, too, in a different way. There is not the time as you know it but there are moments of understanding that there are certain structures pertaining to levels of conscious awareness. As all of the ones we perceive as leaving earth dimension can choose to re-enter into another body or move into higher learning in realms beyond the physical. Many choose to be in body to help other souls reach the awareness of other dimensions in body. This is all for each individual soul and the contracts of group souls.

My life span in a body was to be of a few years and if the ones choosing to be with me in body would have awakened in a more conscious way, then it was my choice to stay or not. The choice was made to leave at this time for the growth of the masses not just for our immediate family. There will be much more expressed to you about this matter.

The understanding of the death will help many. The continuation of my own understanding will help you. There are no doubts in the mind of the heart. The heart chooses to not blame anyone especially yourselves. The fear that is developed from the thoughts of unlovingness is the greatest tragedy of all. There may be a celebration in hearts when human kind understands the perfection of all events in life and the release of pain and suffering need not be a life long experience. The struggles around death are only created by the mind that does not believe in the truth of living Spirit.

God is the experience that Heaven is. It's all Heaven even on earth if one chooses to live present in the heart. The expression of hell is a place where humans put themselves because they cannot face the thought of being in total oneness with God, losing their own ego description of self.

There are many opportunities for you now to remember the gifts of our moments together in earthly bodies and know that it is all energy living on in everything you will ever know. Forgive yourselves for the moments you forgot that you were heaven and let yourself be this space for many souls who are searching for the moment of remembering. There is only 'One' and together the truth will free all to be creating what I am in Spirit.

Sam in Spirit

I love you

After I finished writing I read the words and then wrote a letter to the Johnsons trying to express what I just had experienced.

Dear Dawn and Tim;

Now as I sit here in the glow of this love I feel in me, I realize what he was doing. He was showing me heaven on earth through his eyes. He is also showing me how multi-dimensional we are. Maybe children have a feeling of it more easily because they can be more present and in imagination. I have sat on this dock many times through my growing up. I have never experienced nature serenade me so loudly and all at once. He was definitely getting my attention to focus fully so that the letter could come through. Now when the letter is finished, nature shares her beauty but it is softer and more spacious. A beautiful morning to know God more in me. I look forward to sharing this gift of thought and experience with you.

Love, Frannie

This experience for the Johnsons was huge. I know that it brought great joy, yet enormous pain as well. They needed time to process as both Tim and Dawn were experiencing tremendous grief. Although I have children of my own, I cannot imagine the pain of losing a child in this way. I hoped that in some way God had used me to bring some peace and understanding to these beautiful people.

During the sessions with Tim and Dawn I did share with Tim that he would write a book one day. A year later he produced *Searching For Sam. A Fathers Quest For Meaning.*

www.searchingforsam.com

30

This Call Is On My Dime

A few days later, my father called to me saying the geese were outside by the dock. It was evening as I went out to visit them. In my heart I could feel Sam and lots of love filled me. Then the phone rang. It was Dawn calling from her home in Alberta, Canada. I was excited to hear from her. She was so honest with her feelings as she told me how she longed to feel Sam and see him like he was before his death; to touch him, to hear him, to smell him, to see him just one more time. As a mother, I would want the same. I felt so much compassion in my heart and was grateful that she shared her appreciation for the work we had done together.

Months later, when I was back in Florida for a brief visit with Luke and Lane, I woke up early to meditate. While I was feeling God loving me with this incredible energy of peace, I asked, what I am to do next and opened myself to any sort of guidance.

During the meditation I began to see a vision of a woman and small children walking down a hallway. It was as if I was right there and I saw it with all of my senses. Then I felt the presence of Sam and he was asking me to call his Mom and tell her his little brother was going to be okay. I was hesitant to call because it was so early in the morning in Alberta.

I continued to feel Sam and he began to show me a book – my book. He told me it was time to write this experience I had with him and his family. I saw it all in my mind's eye and it all made sense to me.

I again felt Sam urge me to call his Mom. I was a bit nervous and wondered if anyone would be awake. Dawn answered the phone and was so happy to hear from me. She told me baby Levi had been sick all through the night and they were worried about him.

I think Sam just wanted us to connect. I also felt it was a sign for me to trust what I hear. I believe it takes courage and faith to trust Spirit this way. I have never been disappointed when I go out on a limb. There is always a reason and eventually it reveals itself to me.

Dawn and I had a wonderful conversation. I heard her faith and energy much stronger than our meeting in the summertime. She shared with me both the anger and happiness she felt during the months that we did not speak. I could feel that she was moving through her grief and was seeing the blessings for herself and her family. As we spoke, I could feel Sam's energy merge with her. Dawn told me Sam visited Tim in his dreams and she wondered why she couldn't experience him in this way.

I told her that I believed she embodied Sam; that his energy became one with hers. I explained that in this way, she anchored Sam's God energy into this dimension through her open heart. Dawn was pure love and I felt the healing as she shared with me. She ended the conversation by saying that whenever I have any experiences with Sam to call and let the charges be reversed so "it's on our dime." As I hung up the phone I could hear loudly inside my mind, "No, it's my dime." I could feel that voice was Sam.

When I got up off the floor, I noticed something shiny where I was just sitting. I reached down and picked up a new Canadian dime. I phoned Dawn back immediately and she said, "Knowing Sam, you watch, this call won't be charged on your phone bill."

There are many reasons why the non-physical world wants to communicate with us. There are so many gifts I receive when I have the courage to take a step forward in sharing the truth. I am not always accurate in my interpretation of what I receive but I believe in the truth and that it will always set us free. Whatever Dawn received from my sharing, is for her. That's how God works. We're the vessels for Spirit.

The call never was charged onto the phone bill. That phone call truly was on Sam's dime.

31

Going to See the Miracle Man In Brazil

I sat across from my friends Bob and Diana, totally engrossed in the details of their personal miracle. I believe in miracles – heck, my whole life has been a miracle! Just being alive is a miracle, which is why I love hearing peoples' personal stories.

Wayne Dyer has been an inspiring teacher for me, not just in his books, but in person, too! His views on the relationship between mindsets and miracles are very much like my own. In his book, *10 Secrets For Success and Inner Peace*, he writes,

> *"For every person who has had spontaneous healings or has overcome something that was considered impossible, the individual went through a complete reversal of personality. They actually rewrote their own agreement with reality. To experience Godlike spontaneous miracles, you must have a sense of yourself as Godlike. The Scripture says, 'With God, all things are possible.'"*[20]

I sat with Bob and Diana knowing they had been changed by a trip to Brazil to be in the presence of a healer called 'John of God' (Joao de Deus). Bob had been diagnosed with a rare retinal disease called serpiginous choroiditis. After thirteen years and five laser surgeries, he was legally blind. I heard about his challenges with his failing eyesight. The last time I saw him, he didn't know who I was until I stood very close to him and spoke. Now I was sharing in Bob's excitement and hope for the miracle of sight after being with this man some have written books about, such as *The Miracle Man*, by Robert Pellegrino-Estrach and *The Book of Miracles: The Healing Work of Joao de Deus*, by Josie Ravenwing.

After listening to Bob and his partner Diana share with me their experience of being in Brazil, I said to myself, "I want to go to stand in front of this man, too!" I believed in miracles and truly wanted to reduce my sensitivities to the environment.

One day I returned to Colleen's house after being out in the world again – I had spent the day in Toronto. It had been a great day and I was very excited and wanted to tell her all about it. But as soon as I began talking, I felt as if I had been punched in my lungs. I took a sudden deep breath and began experiencing a severe chemical reaction. At that moment, Colleen remembered she had cleaned a part of the carpet with a chemical spray earlier in the day, never dreaming the chemicals would still be gassing out so many hours later.

I went directly to Karen's home, a mutual friend. She had a sauna, which usually helped me recover more quickly and easily. Karen took one look at me and said, "I'm sending you to Brazil to be with that healer!" My dear friend Karen, with her generous, loving heart, gifted the trip to me.

A few weeks later, I was on a plane with one of my angel sisters, Kathy. We went with Josie Ravenwing, who had experienced healings herself and was now bringing groups down from all over the U.S.A.

The Casa de Dom Inacio, in Abadiania, Brazil is a holy site where you instantly feel at peace upon entering the property. Hundreds come to stand in front of the healer Joao each day and he never turns anyone away. This man has devoted his life to being a medium. He incorporates into his work over thirty entities that were physicians, theologians and therapists during their lifetime on earth, allowing them to take over his body. Healing is a personal process, whether it's physical, emotional, mental, spiritual or any combination of these. I saw some people who had instantaneous healings and others who were slower in their recovery.

We were initially asked to sit in a current room – a room filled with energy because so many people are meditating and bringing in energy. When I entered, I saw many people sitting on benches meditating and heard music playing. I immediately recognized the music – "Brother Sun, Sister Moon." This song always touched me in a special place because of my connection to St. Francis of

Assisi. The energy was very strong. I sat quietly, feeling the current of energy move through my body.

As I enjoyed the peace and quiet of my mind, I connected with my Grandma, whose name was Frances. The last time I had been with her before this trip, she hugged me with all of her physical strength. From her soft loving heart she said, "I wish I could give you my strong, healthy body." At the time she was ninety-eight years old and for her whole life she had been very healthy both in mind and body. She also loved to travel and see the world. She added, "I won't be traveling anymore, Frannie. Take me with you in your heart and I will see the world through your eyes."

I heard her words again in the current room, just before I was ushered into the next room. As I walked in, my body began to vibrate uncontrollably. I began to cry, as love entered my heart. In that moment, I knew I was being healed.

We walked into another room where Joao was sitting and seeing each person individually. I stood in front of Joao asking within my heart to have a healing of my physical body. Standing in front of him, I felt the presence of an impersonal God as he spoke to me in Portuguese. The translator then told me that I would have psychic surgery later that day.

I was told to sit in the same room where I had been with Joao earlier that day. As he began his work, the energy moved up and down my spine. I felt I was having a life review. Events and experiences of my life, ones I had never even thought of since they happened, moved through my mind. It was like watching a mini-movie of my life.

When it was time for the psychic surgery, all of us - men, women and children - were brought into another room together. I felt as if I was under an anesthetic - they called it Spiritual anesthesia. We all closed our eyes as Joao came in and spoke. The energy of the room heightened with his presence and the light in my mind's eye spiraled all colors in this experience. Then it began. It felt as if someone was tugging inside my abdomen. The whole event lasted for about half an hour, though it felt like just a few minutes. After it was over, I went outside and sat under a tree. I heard a voice, which told me that the area where my fallopian tubes (I had them tied after my daughter's birth fourteen years earlier) was unblocked.

I went back to my hotel room to rest, thinking I had received an energy healing, not a physical healing. But later when I woke up, my abdomen was swollen and very tender, as if I had really had surgery. That night in my dream, my dad came to me crying about Grandma. He said to me, "It's so hard to let her go."

When I returned from Brazil, I found out that while I was away, my Grandma had fallen and broken her hip. She was in such bad shape she needed surgery and my dad had to sign a letter requesting no life support if something happened. Her physical surgery took place at the same time I was having my psychic surgery. Everyone was relieved when she came through the operation without many complications.

Afterwards, my family saw such a change in her. She was softer and more loving – my family said she now sounded more like me! Perhaps that is why I thought of her before my healing – and maybe we both helped each other at this moment while we both were being healed.

I loved the experience in Brazil. The group I was with became a safe place for my healing and united me with more soul family. Many of us continue to remain connected with each other in some way.

I returned to Florida for a few months to visit with my children and with Steve. One day, as I was sitting on the beach, I felt the presence of a Spirit that wanted to be born. I knew Steve wanted a baby and a part of me wondered if I could ever conceive again. I knew I was willing, yet I did not really think I was physically capable.

That night as I slept beside Steve, I dreamt that this Spirit from the beach spoke to me, loudly telling me, "I'm coming now! I'm coming Mommy and Daddy!" I woke up to find Steve making love to me while he was sleeping. I stopped him immediately, saying, "No, I could get pregnant!" I thought I had had an energy healing in Brazil, but Spirit was telling me something different. Besides, after the surgery I had in Brazil, I was told not to have sexual intercourse for thirty days.

I didn't think much about it again until a month later. My cycle was late and I was feeling nauseous. Soon after, I experienced a miscarriage a few days before I had to go back to Canada. I had indeed become pregnant that night. I believe the spirit of this baby wanted to come to earth, but my body was not able to bring it into the world. Still, I was living proof that believing in something truly creates an opportunity for miracles. This experience showed me how powerful I can be at creating a miracle, because I am so open to the possibilities.

I felt the healing I received by standing with "John of God." I felt my connection to my power and the strength to accept my life as it was, but not to give up my dreams. I remember sitting in the current room in Brazil, asking God what to do in my relationship with Steve. God answered, "Just love him."

So I went back to Canada holding my dreams of being back in Florida and letting go of the outcome. I became more focused in my work and life in Toronto and began planning a second trip to Brazil. Kathy and I decided to hold a retreat in Brazil. She organized it, and in the spring we took twenty men and women with us to experience their own healings.

My experience with John of God helped me on more levels than I could truly appreciate. I came away from that experience with a knowing that I could heal my body. The entities that spoke through Joao strongly encouraged me to forgive and let go of the past. I finally got the connection – we feed our bodies with these healing thoughts.

From talking to many others who experienced this healer, I heard the entities would say over and over again, "to know you are healed," to believe in your own process. Healing did not always mean the physical body would be healed. I met a blind man who was told his eyesight would never return, but that he would develop his inner eyesight. There were so many stories to tell. They are all so different; yet in so many ways the same. There are certain people that choose to serve in this huge way. Joao de Deus is a medium for Spirit to guide us all to our own healing. I believe no one can be healed unless we choose it. As Wayne Dyer says, "You'll see it when you believe it!"[21]

As for my friend Bob, from the beginning of this chapter... his vision is now healed. He and Diana regularly take groups to Brazil so people can have the chance to heal, like Bob. The Western world may say, "there is no more hope," but in truth, where there is love, there is always hope.

(www.miraclesofjohnofgod.com)

32

Balance In All My Bodies
Is Heaven On Earth

"The Doctor of the future will give no medicine, but will interest his patients in care of the human frame, in diet and in the cause and prevention of disease." –Thomas Edison

To support me in the healing of this physical body I need a doctor who is aligned with my vision. I don't want to mask the symptoms, I choose to find and eliminate the causes of the problems. I think it is important for the treatment to improve health and function of body systems without taxing it. This is where we, as individuals, must get to know our own body's barometer and limitations.

Dr. James Martin, a clinical nutritionist who operates a holistic family practice in Sarasota (The Martin Clinic 800-222-3610), is one of the doctors who has supported me this way. Even though I had been detoxifying my body for many years and addressing the causes of some of the symptoms, I still could be affected by exposure to certain chemicals, which could cause severe reactions. My belief, that too many toxins in the body can cause disease, is supported by Dr Martin. In his book, *New Advances in Natural Health & Healing*, he writes:

"When it comes to traditional, conventional medicine, the different symptoms are viewed as different body parts being ill. What if all these symptoms are interrelated? What if your headache, skin rash, constipation, stomach ulcer, insomnia and muscle spasms are all symptoms of the same underlying problem?

What if the medicines that suppress your pain also can suppress your immune system and possibly compromise your health over the long term?

Most symptoms are the body's way of trying to get rid of toxins and to regain homeostasis and balance. Therefore, most diseases should be treated not by suppressing the body's defense mechanisms, but by cooperating with these systems.

Toxins may be defined as substances that produce physical, emotional and psychological imbalances in an individual. We are constantly exposed to toxins every day. There are two types of toxins: exogenous and endogenous. Exogenous toxins are present in the outside environment, whereas endogenous toxins are produced as a result of imbalances in our metabolism.

The gradual accumulation of low levels of toxins cannot yet be measured by conventional analytical methods; so many doctors deny their existence. As instrumentation and measuring methods become more sophisticated, such toxic states will be recognized as dangerous."[21]

Dr. Martin has developed a sensitive tool, NutraScan, which can detect these toxins and their whereabouts in the body (www.nutritionscan.cc).

I started to have many symptoms of toxicity at a very young age, but failed to recognize the signs. This toxicity led to chronic damage to certain internal organs and tissues. Since I was born as a multiple and so small at birth, I think my immune system was compromised right from the beginning of my life. I was a very sickly child. I believe the body is a very powerful detoxifier but excessive stresses or chronic illness can slow the process down. Any disease or excessive stress can compromise the body's ability to detoxify, resulting in a body that is overloaded with toxins.

I was overloaded at times and often physically ill. I was detoxifying but not properly. As a result, I was not actually cleansing my body. Instead of leaving my body, the toxins resettled in the same or different tissues, which caused more reactions. When detoxifying, the cells get stimulated and begin to release toxins. You need your immune system to draw upon the resources of the body in order to eliminate them.

When the main toxins are eliminated, most organs and tissues will heal and repair themselves. Proper nutrition, diet and supplements support the body in repairing and healing itself. I learned through my healing experiences that each person has a unique toxic load profile with different associated symptoms. I had to get to know my body and set boundaries for myself as I continued to heal. What I still needed to see more clearly was that unresolved emotions could become overpowering and draining on the body, too!

My toxic reactions left me feeling vulnerable and emotional. When the mind keeps you stuck in the emotional body as a victim of the experience, your attachment can keep you toxic. The body is so weakened by the emotional toxicity, that it feels physically drained all the time. This seemed to be a pattern for me – I would become unbalanced emotionally, as well. Balance is important in all areas of our life. Whether we leave our emotions and don't deal with them or we stay stuck in them because we feel victimized, imbalance in our emotional bodies can cause imbalance in our physical bodies.

I see the importance of healing all of our bodies. Whether we start with the physical or the emotional, either path will bring us to more of ourselves. We must know when we are still plugged into our past and recognize when our personal history is not feeding us. These experiences are not of love. Our immune system is strongest when we are in the state of love and gratitude.

I continued to live in the world believing I had healed my past wounds, yet subconsciously I was keeping them alive. There was still more for me to see. *A Course In Miracles* teaches us to see everything outside of ourselves without labeling it, to see it as if for the first time.

For example, when you are sitting beside a tree, is it anything but a tree? Do you ask the tree to be a certain way so that you can feel love? Suppose when you look at the tree you think about the last time you sat under that tree – with an ex-boyfriend. All the painful thoughts about that relationship come to you and you begin to feel the pain. Whenever you are with the tree, will you feel these uncomfortable feelings? Is the moment feeding you? Or will you unplug and feel the power of creation in that very moment? You can, if you make a conscious choice to do so.

It doesn't mean that you hide the feeling. It means that you recognize that your feeling brings you to a thought that can be healed. The power of the moment is yours to tap into. The moment is allowing you to source your own personal power, which is God power. This energy is the healer. The healer stands in the center of her heart and is not attached to the present or the future. The healer is the impersonal God.

I had a dream where I was my mother, who was very sick and distorted like Linda Blair in *The Exorcist*. That is how I feel when I am ill and shut down. At the same time in this dream, I was a healer standing before my mother. I felt the power of my Spirit. Knowing I was the healer, I raised my arms above her and waved my hand and said, "With the power of the Holy Spirit, YOU ARE HEALED!" At that moment, all the darkness moved out of me and light dissolved the moment. I woke up and felt this energy physically moving through me.

A Course In Miracles says, "Health is the remembrance that illusions are not real."[22] Within myself, I have the power to choose to let go of thoughts that do not feed me. Each of us can create an inner reality of peace and be clear in the moment of our own personal power. In this moment I am okay just as I am, whether or not my body is disabled or sick in any way. Thinking that I was not okay was the illusion.

The moment can inspire me, when I am plugged into my creative energy, to make choices from love to support me, just the way I am right now. I am in a human body and my Spirit is full. The feeling of this unconditional love is the healing. If we are not attached to thoughts that keetp us in pain and suffering, then this moment has an opportunity to change. I can choose to experience myself as whole and complete, just as I am. This is my power and this is where I can step into my life and create a whole new world for me to live in. This is the place that God intended for us all to experience – Heaven on earth in a body.

33

Letting Go To Experience
Truth In The Moment

From Colleen's home just west of Toronto, I drove up north to visit my parents at their summer home near Owen Sound, Ontario. The two and a half hour drive was like a meditation, watching nature as I witnessed the change of seasons – something I had missed while living in Florida for twelve years. It felt good to get out of the big and busy city.

Traffic was non-existent on this sunny Saturday morning and I enjoyed driving and being with myself. It was like a therapy session as I let my mind release all the clutter of different thoughts accumulated. I became an unattached listener.

Years of meditating and journaling have brought me this wonderful gift. I experience many different feelings and emotions and without denying them, I don't stay stuck in any one of them. My conscious breath continues to bring me back to my heart and into a space of emptiness.

It doesn't have to be a phenomenon, like a fiery bush, for you to feel or hear God (not to say those things don't happen). I used to think I had to meditate and be in an altered state to experience the dynamics of Spirit. Now I realize the subtle existence of God in the simple moments of living here on the earth in this body.

As I was driving, I noticed a sign on the side of the road that said, 'Honey for Sale.' I then saw a vision of my sister-in-law Marion, who had passed away four years before. In my mind, I suddenly saw her making honey. At that very instant my body was consumed with a vibration of energy that began moving throughout my body. The energy was so strong I felt I wanted to cry with the immense feelings of love. My heart was open and my mind was empty as I felt Marion's safe and familiar presence. I believed I was tapped into my higher self, as energy communicated truth to guide me.

I do not remember word for word what I heard, but as I listened, I let it merge with me. I spoke the words out loud in the silence of my car. At times like this, I wished I had my tape recorder handy but these meetings with our Spirit loved ones are not always planned.

As I tuned into the experience, I embraced the truth communicated through me and for me. I don't know how I drove the car because I was so focused on this experience, but I did. What I received I already knew intellectually, yet now as I embodied the energy, I wanted to live the truth that the words conveyed:

"Every moment, every experience up to this moment has brought you here. In this moment all of this energy and truth is available to you. All this energy can move into your future. This energy is your partner, your work, your home and your health. All this energy is for you. Be it now. Nothing can hold you back. Letting go of the past will give you the freedom to be all that you are right now. It is up to you to share it as you be it."

The energy was physically vibrating my body and the flow of love was powerful. In that moment, I felt the freedom in letting go of the life I had been living in Florida.

A few hours after I arrived at the cottage, I went for a jog around the lake. I came across something on the side of the road – and upon investigation, discovered what looked to me like a big white goose. It had been shot in the neck. She was still alive and I could tell she was in shock and maybe her neck was broken.

I sat close, asking in my heart, "what can I do?" I was a bit cautious because I wondered if I should touch it or not. Would she defend herself by biting me? Am I going against nature? Should I just let it die?

Well, I just sat and prayed, looking into the goose's eyes. The bird lay still as I listened inside for guidance, holding the space for her. Intuitively I felt it was okay for me to stroke the goose on its head and I continued to pray for guidance. Waiting patiently, I heard the voice inside from God say, *"Heal all creatures. Take time to touch all of my creations."*

Without hesitation, I picked up this 25-pound animal in one arm, while with the other hand I held the goose's damaged neck and began walking back to the cottage on the lake. The bird did not resist, but lay comfortably in my arms as if it trusted me to help her.

As I walked up the porch step with this beautiful bird, I saw my dad who came quickly to the door. He thought I should put it out of its misery. I said, "No, I believe I can help it either in its transition into Spirit or by sharing energy to help it get stronger, to heal." I said to myself, "I work at Hospice house with the dying and this is no different."

I put the bird on towels and she did not resist me at all. It was a safe place for the goose to be as I continued to pray and asked to be a vessel for God's healing energy. I have learned to let go of any expectations in the outcome of sharing energy and the most important lesson for me is to let go and allow myself to be the safe space for healing.

As I laid my hands on the goose, the same energy I had felt when I experienced Marion's presence surged through me. Slowly with each surge of energy, the bird lifted its neck a little more. My Dad stood beside me watching this event.

After about an hour, I felt the strength in the bird as it sat up erect and stood on its legs. I watched as it instinctively went towards the water but of course it didn't know the window was in its way. I carried her outside feeling the excitement and strength in this huge bird as she stretched out her wings. Standing together, my Dad and I cheered it on. As we watched, we realized this bird was not a goose at all, but a beautiful white swan. Tears of joy moved through us as we watched the swan make her way to the lake ahead. The healing was as much for my father and me, as it was for the injured bird.

Later that evening my brother Phil called me. After I shared the experiences of the day, he told me something very interesting that happened at this time of year, four years ago - just before Marion died. Phil and Marion had found a Canada goose that had been shot and my brother plucked it and cooked it for dinner. As he was talking, those familiar truth chills were moving through my body. He told me Marion had become very sick that night after eating the wild game and as Phil looked back at that night, to him it was 'The Last Supper.'

From that moment on, Marion began spiraling downwards to her death. They had to take her to the emergency room, where she was hospitalized and died soon after. What kind of coincidence was this, I wondered? What was Marion trying to communicate to me today in the car? For me, it was about living Spirit. The bird had a choice to stay in a body or not. Marion left her physical body, but that same energy, as Marion, is still alive. It's alive in me, it's alive in the swan and it's alive in every moment we choose to be present. It's in every moment of existence and we can tap into it in every moment if we choose to be conscious of it. This energy is our life force and it is always present; with or without the body this energy is still alive. This incredible power is in us right this moment. If we choose to let go and let the past die, the present can rebirth the truth of who we are today. This is freedom to be. This energy can be birthed into anything, anyone and anywhere. It's tricky because ego wants to continually attach to the past. As we let go and trust, like the swan, all the power is available for this moment to create the future. Whatever the future will be.

The swan lived on the lake for over a year. The story touched the hearts of many who lived on Lake McCullough, who watched throughout the following year and made sure the swan had a safe place to continue its healing.

34

The White Limousine

When I walked into the hospital room in Tampa, Florida, I had just received the news that the surgeon could not help my friend, Ann St. Ives. When he opened her up, she was so full of cancer he just closed her back up again. There was nothing he could do. Ann said she wanted quality of life instead of quantity and whatever they could do to help her with the pain would be great.

It was amazing what went through my mind when I first saw her lying in bed. What could I say to her to make her feel better? That part of me that wants to heal and make life a little easier told me to be strong. Another part of me was already crying inside, angry the verdict was so severe. I looked at her and as she opened her eyes and saw me, the love radiated in every cell of my body. I felt so much love for her and in that moment I knew all I needed to be was me. I wanted to hold the space for Ann in whatever way I could. As she shared her feelings with me, I didn't stop the tears that flowed down my cheeks. I knew I was in the presence of courage, for she had always been that to me. Yet, as she allowed me to do some energy work in silence, I could sense she was tired and did not want to think about anything. So, together in silence we felt God embracing us here in this world. There was nothing to say right now and so we simply felt the love.

When her sister Gillian arrived, we talked about miracles and how we believed in them. Earlier that day I had been swimming with manatees and I felt their beautiful message to us was, "*just be.*" I wanted to share their message with Ann, so I picked up a crystal with a manatee on it and brought it to Ann's room. "Rest now Ann," I said as we left, "and let us all show you how much we love you."

Ann was an artist. The walls of her little beach house on Manasota Key were filled with her paintings of the ocean, animals and places she had visited or lived. The colors were vibrant and so alive and passionate. She had moved to Florida after attending one of my meditation groups. She had lived in the Virgin Islands for a long time and I think she found a community of women here that she felt comfortable with. The power of women's circles has always been important for my growth and I was grateful to share my home with all those who wanted to grow Spiritually.

After her diagnosis Ann became even more loving. I witnessed this remarkable woman impart her wisdom in her dying process as she shared honestly with those who were blessed to spend time with her. One day she gave me a beautiful hand-painted sarong that I longed to wear. There it was, just sitting in my donation bowl after one of our meditation group gatherings. She was so sweet and so humble as she shared herself with me.

Now I was back in Canada, talking to her on the telephone and knowing any day she would make the transition from her body. It was difficult to hear all the words she was speaking; yet the truth that moved through her gave me goose bumps with every word. She was already beyond her body and letting go of this world. She was so brave and so truthful as she talked about the challenge of coping with the physical pain in her body.

Ann said she wanted to hold on a little longer until her sisters and mother arrived from England on December twentieth. That was two weeks away. She was surrendering though, as she shared that she knew she was no longer her body. She wasn't afraid of death and actually looked forward to the freedom from the body.

Ann thanked me for helping her open up to her own self-love and her own energy. As she prepared for her departure, she appreciated everyone in her life and felt so blessed. We talked about being together one more time. I assured her I would be with her during her transition, even if I could not be with her physically. To be able to speak so honestly with her at this time was such a gift for me and so freeing. Even though we were speaking by telephone, the power in her presence touched me deeply. She had no fear of dying and was fully in love in her last conscious moments. How blessed I was to speak to her this last time while she was in her body.

Later that day, I went to see an apartment I thought for sure would be my new home. I had looked at it from the outside the night before with my girlfriend Joey. We even climbed onto the roof next door to look into the rooms from the outside. Although I had the first and last month's rent with me, I now had an odd feeling I would not take it. The feeling in my solar plexus was not pleasant as the landlord, named Steve, took me around. I saw a hole in the ceiling, paint peeling off the walls and the old basement floor, where I would have to do my laundry, was dirt. I could not feel happy in this place. It wasn't what I wanted and I could not bring myself to fully commit to it. I listened to my inner voice and decided not to give him the money. Instead, I said I would contact him later.

As I left the area, which is called The Beaches in east Toronto, I felt relieved but sad. I wanted to find a home for myself before Luke and Lane came to spend Christmas with me. I wanted to find my own space to prove to myself that I was moving forward with my life in Canada. But this apartment was just not for me and I was grateful I had not taken it out of fear of not finding the perfect place to call home. I was still certain I would be taken care of as long as I listened to what I felt was true for me.

As I drove back to Colleen and Bruce's home, I was very connected to my feelings. A song came on the radio that reminded me of Steve back in Florida. I missed him so much and longed for my life to be with his. Then a white limousine drove by and it triggered memories that touched my grief and the tears started to flow. I cried for Ann. I cried for Steve and me. I cried for my daughter and I cried to be back in Florida again. When I arrived home, I cried with my sister. Where had all these tears come from, I wondered? I thought I had let go of Steve. Maybe my friend Ann who was dying helped me to feel more of my own tears. More letting go of what was, so that this new life could be birthed.

I have another dear friend called Ann who has lived a courageous life challenged with migraine headaches. I called her and shared my feelings about the grief of parts of me that were dying; the letting go of living in Florida near my daughter; and the letting go of being with Steve. I loved him and I was angry that we weren't together. I told her I didn't want to keep loving him, but I did. I felt it was easier to be angry. Ann began to speak from her heart and she said, "All the feelings are real...they are all okay. You can get on with your life and still love Steve."

Her wisdom inspired me that night as she shared truth with me. She helped me remember that I could still love Steve, for our love is of the heart. I hung up the phone feeling inspired and remembering I do not have to judge any of my feelings. I had been judging myself for my angry feelings, like when in my hurt I had yelled at Steve the day before, "Why haven't you sold my car yet?"

All these feelings were okay – my feelings, Ann St. Ives' feelings. Ann had shared her pain of how hard it was to be in a body that is in pain; yet she felt the vastness and the love of Spirit more than ever before. To be with all of the parts of our self and judge none is to be the master.

That night, I fell asleep easily and awoke a couple of hours later to use the bathroom. On my return to bed, I tripped over the phone and knocked the receiver off the cradle. I heard no dial tone. When I picked it up, there was silence.

"Hello?" I queried and then a voice began to speak. To my amazement, it was Steve.

"The phone never rang," I said, " I just picked it up."

"That's how connected we are," he replied.

He had called to tell me he had sold my car and then out of the blue he asked me to come to Florida tomorrow; he would pay for my ticket. Somewhat taken aback I asked him, "Why?" He said he missed me terribly. He wanted to touch me again. Then he said, "Frannie, don't go to your head. What does your heart say?" Without hesitation I said, "My heart misses you and wants to touch you and see you and feel you." He urged me to book a flight right away before our minds told us all the reasons not to see each other.

I went to sleep asking for a message from Spirit to show me if it was in my highest good to go to Florida and see Steve again. When I woke up in a dream at dawn, I saw my girlfriend Judy coming from the light and saying, "Go with your heart, it will never betray you."

In my meditation that morning, the guidance I received was that the opening could be behind me or in front of me. To know that life is one big adventure. Can I go to Steve without assuming anything? I was excited to reunite with him and what a blessing it would be to see Ann before she transitioned. I believed my dying friend had a large part to play in this trip, for Steve later told me that when he called that night, he'd had no intention of asking me to come to him.

As Colleen drove me to the airport, the song that reminds me of Steve came on the radio. Then Colleen said, "Watch for the white limousine." At that moment a white limousine pulled alongside us and escorted us to the airport. Colleen blurted out, "Steve is going to ask you to marry him!" I did not think that was even remotely possible. I was going to see my friend Ann St. Ives before she passed away. I believed she had made this all happen so I could see her one last time in a body. I did not know why I was going to see Steve again. I just knew that I loved him.

There is a bit of a story around the white limousine. About two years prior, Colleen was visiting me in Florida. We were driving to Sarasota when a white limousine pulled up beside us. At that moment I started to see a vision in my third eye that would not leave. I had to pull to the side of the road. I shared with Colleen that I had seen Steve and me being married. Why did I see this vision at this time? It always stayed with me as some kind of omen. When I was with Steve and feeling insecure about our relationship, many times the white limo would be near us. I never shared with

Steve what the vision was, only that it was a sign of some sort. It always got both our attention.

When the plane landed, it was our song that was blaring through the intercom. I felt a bit nervous. When I walked through the gate, I saw him standing there and as we walked slowly towards one another the past dissolved. As our bodies met, we were one in the love that has always been. It was like a new relationship. I witnessed and felt myself very present in the moment.

When I called Ann St. Ives, her sister Gillian answered the phone. She told me that Ann was in a coma. Gillian was so pleased I called and that I was in Florida. She thanked me for helping Ann find love because in her words, "life had made Ann a prickly pear." Gillian also told me how the day before she had gone to the funeral home to make arrangements and the owner asked if she was from England. He said he was from a place called St. Ives. Gillian was so excited knowing how divine even Ann's dying was. I asked her to whisper in Anne's ear and tell her that I am here and that I'll be coming soon to be with her. But it was only minutes later that Ann died and I was not able to see her or touch her in her body again.

A few days later while I was driving, Ann came to me in Spirit. Her truth moved so powerfully through my body as I felt her love and she spoke to my heart. *"You showed me the love again,"* she said, *"and I am helping you to remember the love you have with Steve. Thank you."* I felt her gift and I thanked her as I cried with joy and celebration of her life and her love. The week with Steve was more than I could have imagined. It felt like all those love movies I had watched in the past, where afterwards I would say, "That only happens in the movies." I felt our open hearts and fell deeper in love with him than ever. At around five o'clock on the evening before I had to leave to go back to Canada, Steve committed to me and said he wanted to marry me.

When I returned to Toronto, Colleen felt the shift in me immediately. "Are you and Steve going to get married?" she asked. "We're talking about it," I replied. She then told me that the night before, at around five in the evening, she was driving with Bruce, her fiancée, and her children. When Colleen noticed a white limousine pull up alongside them, she said, "Maybe Steve is asking Frannie to marry him right now!" Then she told them all the story of the white limousine. By the time she finished the story, two more white limousines were driving beside them! Three white limousines in total.

Was it all just a coincidence?

On May 4, 2001 a white limousine picked Steve and me up at his home on the Gulf of Mexico and took us to the beach where our family and friends had gathered for our wedding. That same summer my sister Colleen married Bruce and later, my brother Phil married his new love, Janine. There were three weddings in our family that summer. And somehow we all felt that they had been accurately predicted by the symbol of the three white limousines that day.

35

Ann St. Ives

I truly believe that through her love, Ann facilitated my reunion with Steve. But that was not her only gift to me. In early January 2001 as I was sitting at the computer, I suddenly felt Ann's presence. As I opened to the energy I was inspired to bring the message that came to the people who knew her. This letter was formed as I typed the words that moved through me.

January 5, 2001

"*Let me tell you what it is like to be in Spirit. Let me help you to understand the mystery that is within each one of you. This is not just for a few. This is for all to recognize as one allows the true nature of being to live in the moments of human life.*

There is an opportunity for you all to breathe into the great vastness of this mystery that you seek to understand. To appreciate that there is only one that is experiencing. It is all God. It is all that can be living within every moment of your conscious existence.

As I am with you, allow these words to embody the love you are searching for. Every step you take upon this earth and in this body is bringing you to your fullest expression. What is this expression? It is who you are and all of you can reveal the mystery that is in you to share with humanity.

If you would like to understand, then allow all of your thinking to cease and feel the emptiness within your mind that begins to uncover your truest feelings of love that is within your heart. These feelings of love are in you always, yet you do not always allow yourself to feel this magnificence. It really is magnificent. It is what you search for outside of yourself. As you allow yourself to touch this and feel this, the world outside begins to be your reflection of this inner state of being.

These words are simple and they are not something that you haven't heard before, yet as a human being, you desire to remember. Every word of love can bring you to remember this feeling of love. The feeling of love can be the love in every word. All of this comes from within. Every part is from within, for this is where it is all created. You are the core of this existence. You are the one that houses this mystery and embraces it within your own personality and feelings and brings this energy into creation for the entire world to participate with. You are the part of the puzzle that can bring the love to humanity.

Whoever is to be a part of this whole with you is part of the mystery. Let go of knowing how it is all to become and be the love that is the mystery of God. This energy knows. This energy is the life force of all creation. In every moment you have the opportunity to feel this love and be the peace of God that joins all of the pieces of the puzzle that form this great and grand mystery.

Everything that I saw through my eyes was seen with my heart as I painted for God so that this energy of Great Spirit could touch the heart of another. The colors that shine on the canvas cannot compare to the true colors of God. The world I am a part of now is what you are becoming in every moment. It is the density of this world upon the earth that covers up the energy that radiates these colors that in an instant can bring the world into their true nature.

I, like many other artists, can feel the colors and designs of God as our hearts embrace the feelings; yet it cannot ever fully be seen by the human eye. The world is not fully ready to see as God sees. Yet as the garment of the body is disrobed, the radiant colors of God and Spirit create the moment where the love remembers, when we as soul remember this mystery called God.

It is all encompassing. It opens this world to the magnificence of creation. So vast is its experience, so beautiful is its picture, so sweet is its feeling, that all of us become one in a holy instant. We are connected to one another with or without bodies. All of creation is breathing together like one cell. There is so much life in this place.

However you choose to interpret this expression is up to you. Through these words I feel you as you feel me. Through these feelings we are radiating the energy and light that God is in this moment. It moves into every moment *that exists, with or without your conscious connection. I am the living paintings that I created. You are a part of its creation each time you gaze upon its splendor. This is how we can all connect and create as one.*

Let yourselves fully feel yourself in every moment of living in the body and it is your own interpretation that will bring you to your self-expression of this mystery. I am the mystery that whispers freely in the wind and into your heart I live. Sharing the love we are, I let go of the world, as I once knew it, so that the world of our creator can be manifested through your existence.

Loving you my darlings...Ann"

Painting by Ann St. Ives

This painting of Road Town Harbor, Tortola Island, British Virgin Islands reflects Ann's view from her balcony. She was drawn to this beautiful island by the peace that surrounded her and inspired her art. But it was her illness and her surrender to the dying of her physical body that enabled Ann to finally experience and embrace that peace which resided inside her Self.

36

Love Is the Greatest Teacher

*"...and the day came when the risk to remain tight in a bud was more painful
than the risk it took to blossom."* –Niccolo Machiavelli (1469 - 1527)

Someone once said to me that while some people have degrees
in education, my pursuits have earned me a degree in love. Maybe
that is what inspires me the most, to love deeper and to love more.
For me that is my priority in life - to go inside to find out where I
can love myself more so I can love life in a deeper way.

I continue to be inspired by my life and to find ways to heal
my physical body and mind. My life's pursuit of love continues to
bring me more understanding of self love and divine God love.

I thought I had conquered my own fears of unworthiness,
abandonment and betrayal. After the many years of embracing,
clearing and cleansing my physical body, I thought the journey to
Self had finally brought an understanding that would allow me to
live the love I had been searching for. All of my dreams seemed to
be coming true in one form or another. Years of commitment to
heal my sick body seemed to be paying off because I finally felt
healthier then ever before and I rejoiced in it. I was now married
to my beloved Steve and living in Florida again. Life was beautiful.

A few months after our honeymoon, I went back to Canada
for my sister's wedding. Steve could not travel with me because he
had ruptured a disc in his lower back. The day after Colleen and
Bruce's ceremony, there was a lightning storm. While I was sitting
on a metal exercise bench, a bolt of lightning hit the ground outside
of the room and the electrical surge went right up my legs and up
through my body. I felt it right through my bones as it went out
through the top of my head. It felt like everything stopped inside
of me, like I was stunned. I felt queasy and weak. I felt something
weird had happened in my heart, but I could not explain it. I did

not think much about it, but when I called my husband, I felt increasingly sicker as I talked on the telephone. I decided to just go to bed, thinking I'd feel better the next day, which, basically, I did.

I got on with my life, returned to Florida and forgot about the incident until several weeks later. During those weeks after the lightning strike, I had many heart palpitations but they would pass. I had experienced this before, yet this time the symptoms felt stronger. Why didn't I listen?

My physical heart was calling for love, but I continued not to hear until one day the pain got so bad I felt like I was having a heart attack. The pain was strong in my chest and going down my arm and it was uncomfortable to breathe. I felt sick to my stomach and I was scared. I called Steve. At moments like this, it is amazing all that goes through your mind. Steve was calm but I knew he was concerned. He called the paramedics because the symptoms did not seem to be abating.

I agreed to let the paramedics come to appease him. After living such a healthy lifestyle for so long, I was in denial that anything could really be wrong with my heart. The paramedics checked me as best they could and then told me to go to the hospital. "The next incident might be too late," they warned.

I listened, but also checked inside. My intuition told me I would be better off home in bed with my husband. So we slept in each other's arms as best we could, waking up a lot in the emotionally and physically uncomfortable moments. I felt incredibly weak and lifeless the next day. The pain was getting worse and my pulse was running high. I called my doctors for support and began the search for answers. Once again, I was discouraged and afraid.

My nutritionist, Dr. Jim Martin took a saliva and urine test to see what was going on in my tissues and organs. In the past I had been detoxing my body with the help of his NutriScan approach. Dr. Martin was also a friend and I trusted him. He had worked with someone who studied lightning-hit patients and felt the incident had affected me greatly by upsetting the electrical system around my heart. I also called Dr. Marc Weinberg, a medical doctor. He was a friend who also had done energy healings with me. When he looked at me he said, "How can I support you?" I felt weak in my physical body and unsure what to do next, so Marc suggested we get a cardiologist's opinion.

Marc feels, as I do, that we can heal our bodies with our connection to Spirit but we need to be grounded here. We live in bodies and we are here to take care of them. In my case, Marc said that meant I needed an eco-cardiogram. Steve and I both felt he was right.

I then asked Marc and Ann, my very close friend who is a massage therapist, to lay their hands on me with the hopes of tapping into some information. I laid on the massage table in her living room and the energy felt so safe and nurturing. I found myself in that place between the worlds. There in the light, I felt my grandmother, my girlfriend Debbie (who had died so many years ago of a brain aneurysm) and many other beings of light. I heard it whispered that my contract was up and I could leave now if I wanted. "No" was my immediate response and then I heard a voice say, "Then you will fix your physical heart."

Once again, I was at a crossroad and it all came down to my own beliefs. This experience, I knew, was going to bring me to more truth about myself. I have learned there are no wrong choices for it will all bring me truth. I can only be who I am right now.

I started to have tests done and the eco-cardiogram showed I had mitral valve prolapse, just like my sister Colleen. The cardiologist told me I could not heal it with alternative methods. He told me it was just getting worn out and one day, when it got to the fourth stage, I would need to get it replaced or I would die. He prescribed medicine, a beta blocker to control the symptoms. He told me the episodes might not happen again for a while, or they might happen every month as the valve continued to deteriorate. He said to me again, with such a strong tone, "You cannot heal it naturally and if YOU don't do something when it gets to the fourth stage, YOU WILL DIE."

Wow!!!! No wonder people go into fear after they hear a severe prognosis from their doctor. But I did not buy his sales pitch. I knew in my heart it was up to me.

First, Dr. Martin tested me for viruses and bacteria in the heart. He believed he could help get my heart healthier again using various nutritional supplements like CoQ10 and olive leaf extract, magnesium citrate, vitamin C and E and lots more. He didn't know if we could fix the valve but he felt he could get it all in balance again. That sounded much more positive to me. Because of my history with chemicals, I was more aligned with doing everything I could to heal myself in a more natural way. Taking a beta-blocker would only mask the symptoms. When times got very tough, I must admit I did try the beta-blocker to see if it might help me through the pain. It actually made me worse. I gained no relief whatsoever but experienced all kinds of other symptoms. My body did not like it at all. It's not that I am into pain, but I went back to using all my resources from my past to help me get stronger in all of my bodies. Some days I was inspired and filled with hope, and some days the pain moved me into my deepest despair.

But in the meantime I felt that to be true to myself, I would look deeper. I would embrace the heart pains and give myself the emotional support I needed. I would clear up the toxins that seemed to keep my heart out of balance. I used different breathing techniques to help generate more energy into my heart area and lungs. I do believe I am here to allow the love to move through my heart and in doing this I must also receive it.

One day as I was feeling the pain deeply on a physical level, I held it with total surrender. Instead of trying to get rid of the pain, I let it be there without judging it or leaving it. As I sat in total acceptance of it, more light and energy embraced me. I felt the tightness in my chest begin to lessen and the light got brighter in my mind's eye. I felt a letting go again just like I used to and realized that since this heart episode, I had not allowed myself to fully let go into the light. As the love flowed in and filled my heart, I was in complete peace. Tears ran down my face. Once again I was letting the love in. I became the fullness of this love and I began to write:

"As I sit with myself, allowing myself to continue to be, I recognize that this pain inspires me. It helps me to search for more – to discover ways to go deeper within my very being. So if that is what it is helping me do, then why do I need it to inspire me? When did I decide that pain was what I needed to be inspired with? I write these words from all the parts of me that exist as the whole of me. In the next breath I can breathe into that vastness which is not connected to my pain, yet it can move me out of the pain.

So I ask the pain what it is?
"I am the fear of love."

Wow, that is quite direct, isn't it? Okay, so if you are the fear of love, how can I be free of you?
"If you can fully accept the fear and know you are afraid of this love, then this would be a great way to connect with me."

Why am I afraid of the love?
"I am created by your mind and since you were a little girl you decided that the love would hurt you so instead you have stopped it from fully being inside of you and you have left yourself to find it."

Why did I think it would hurt me?
"Because you were so full of love and light that many would come to you to fix them and instead of sharing it, you decided to take on the pain of everyone that was needy of love."

Where did I learn this?
"You learned it from the world you were born into."

How can I open my heart to the love that is here for me?

"Let it hold you just as you are"

In doing this can I heal my physical heart?
"You are healing your physical heart for you are choosing to change your mind about life and death."

Do I need to do anything else?
"You can reach inside and tell me how you want to share this love."

I desire to live in love and peace in every moment of my life in this body and beyond. I choose to be with all of me that is afraid to let love in and FREE myself.
"So be it. In this moment now, you are pure love."

     I continue to ponder these thoughts and wonder if my "pursuit" of love is what I felt all the time, instead of fully allowing the love in when I found it... Maybe I just know how to give love and to receive love has been my challenge. Isn't it everyone's challenge? I contemplate this thought deeper, as I feel what it is like to fully receive the love.

     As I reflect on the lightning hit, I feel it was divine. Instead of believing its power brought me out of balance, I can see it as divine intervention. The experience brought me to what was already out of balance in me: I was giving more than receiving the energy of love for myself. My heart has been starving for my own affection and nurturing. We can talk about love until the cows come home but can we fully realize it within our own self? We are here to be love. Love is the experience of fully being with ourselves without judgment. Love is all that we are.

     Okay, okay, all this love stuff is just words. We can know it all in our mind and babble about love yet how can we define it? Love is this experience we are in a body for. To experience who we are. Everything has opposites so we can experience it. The opposite of love is fear. If we didn't touch our fears, how would we even know that there was love to touch? If we didn't feel love we wouldn't know what we were wanting in our lives. Experiencing is why we have chosen to be in a body. We, as soul, are all-knowing and all-seeing divine beings. We are trying to experience and remember our true identity in these bodies. These bodies allow us as soul, to be in this physical dimension.

All that is our life is touched by Spirit for that is who we are. As soul, I know who I am. It is the body that is remembering who we are. We are here to be all that we are in every moment and this takes being present. Our true nature is pure love.

The truth I am here to remember is that everything I need is within me. This energy of soul, my Spirit, my God is a power I can tap into at any time. The resistance is the mind's fear that keeps me in pain. The leap of faith is to trust more. To have greater faith not just in God but in myself.

I have another physical challenge so I can live the truth of my heart. This energy of love is the healer as I accept this moment as it is and surrender it all to God. Will my body heal? Yes, it is healing. I believe in my own innate Spirit. This power, this love sustains me. I get tired of the physical symptoms but it is the catalyst to bring me to the ultimate truth that I am here to trust in myself as I trust in God. Every breath I take, every step I make is all perfect for me to blossom.

37

Evolution of Communication With Spirit

When I felt I needed guidance, I would sometimes write a question at the top of a blank page, then empty myself fully and wait for an answer. Most of the time, words would simply flow through my pen and onto the page. It was all energy forming the words. When done, it was just like getting a letter in the mail that someone else had written. Even my penmanship would change. I have gotten to the point that I often recognize the guide that is present from what I have written.

This experience helped me to be silent and to listen to my Higher Self. Putting the words on paper anchored the message in a tangible form so I could read it again and understand another way to perceive my questions.

These letters from Spirit then began to come to me in the middle of the night. I would wake up to a voice saying, "Frannie..." It was like someone just walked into the room and whispered in my ear. I'd wake up with a jolt out of my sleep. No one would be there in person or body, but I would clearly feel the presence of someone standing there. It's sort of like having your eyes closed, yet you can feel it when someone is looking at you or entering the room.

I remember my resistance. I would think, "I want to go back to sleep." Sometimes it felt as if hands were pushing me up, out of bed. I would feel that fear of the unknown, the mystery of wondering what is going to happen next.

Now that I am conscious and trusting of my connection to Spirit, I no longer need the prompting and encouragement to engage with the energy. My desire to do my work enables me to stay open and aware of it. Then, as now, the process is the same. I begin by just letting my pen write and it is as if my hand becomes someone else's. The writing is automatic. As I write, I feel the presence and in this feeling I often see visions, or just experience who it is, whether it is an angel, a master teacher or someone who has died.

One of the first letters I brought in from the non-physical world was from a man named Michael to his wife Haike. Haike was a childhood friend who in her twenties lost her husband in a tragic car accident. On the evening of the accident, she had gone to sleep knowing Michael was at a business meeting. At around midnight she was awakened by a strong wind, even though her bedroom window was not open. She later told me that she felt so much anger upon awakening that she began pounding pillows to express her frustration and upset. A little while later, police arrived at her door informing her that her husband was dead. She believed his spirit had come to her when he died and that is why she woke up angry and upset.

Years later I had an experience with Michael in Spirit. I felt a whoosh of energy move through my body and then I felt a presence sit on the bed. The bed actually sunk in as if a physical body was sitting on it. It's difficult to explain, but I had a knowingness that this energy was Michael. I picked up a pen and wrote this letter as his energy moved through me:

My Beloved Haike,

Let me write to you the words you do not hear from me. Let your heart be open to share in the many lessons I am learning on the other side.

It is only the time in your world that matters but here there is no time. But together we share so much that it would be very difficult for your conscious mind to understand all.

It may not sound like these words are coming from me yet if you open yourself up to me, the love will flow through you like never before.

A part of you has closed the doors to love since I left you alone in the physical world. I will never be away from you.

On many levels I do walk but a part of me is always with you. I am helping many to open to their own true self and to be able to feel their own love.

It was a hard time for me when I left my body for the touch of you seemed so difficult to be without. Yet I have so much more with you. We are together as one as we make love in the heavens. You do spend much time at night helping many to heal their hearts.

You must take the love I send to you and open up those doors for others. We will never be truly apart from one another. You are my soul mate and as we fly together know that you are my true love and we will heal many hearts.

Open yourself to the gifts you have. The move for you will open many doors to your true talents. You will get many messages in your dream state. Begin to recognize these gifts you have.

I speak to you through the written word yet I am always by your side when you need the peace of love. I work through you to keep the torch of love alive.

Kissing you with my heart,
Michael

When Haike received this letter she had already remarried and moved on in her new life. While she was happy in her life with her loving husband Ian and their two children, some place deep inside of her still needed to have healing. I believe Michael was helping Haike let go of feelings that blocked her from letting love more fully into her own heart.

Letters that come through like this provide a confirmation for the ones left behind that their departed loved ones are okay. They receive a great deal of comfort in knowing their spirit loved ones are watching over them like guardian angels. I, too, benefit from these experiences. By serving as an open vessel to bring in messages from Spirit, I have learned a great deal and have gained insight into what it may be like beyond the physical realm.

I remember the night I was pushed (or pulled) out of bed by John. John was the husband of Joan, a woman I had modeled with back in Toronto. I had not seen them for quite some time and I knew John had died a few months earlier. As I wrote, John's words flowed through me. It was six o'clock in the morning when I finished and then John pushed me to call Joan. I was unsure – she did not know this part of me – yet the presence was sure this was the time to connect. Sure enough, Joan answered the phone saying she was looking at old photographs and actually had a picture of me in her hand!

Her husband John wanted to touch her from this place where he was now and I was the lucky one he chose to deliver his gift. I felt love and truth in the messages being relayed through me. I was learning to trust these moments and in the end I also learned I had to let go of the outcome. What I do believe is the words I write and the information that comes through me is meant to be shared and may inspire the world we live in.

Those who have walked the earth before us or those that have been in our lives can still inspire us. Their voices are speaking to us from another place. These great souls have left this material world and even without bodies, their spirits are with us, guiding and co-creating with us. This way of receiving information and guidance is the experience of being in your open heart as you surrender to the moment. I know it is a way of life for me as it inspires me to bring in wisdom that is timeless. Through the creative process we all are tapping into that place where time stands still and we are the bridge between the worlds.

Channeling is something we all do when we are completely present in the moment, connected to all of our bodies and all realms that exist beyond this dimension. It is in that moment when we become so empty from our past and our future, that the moment bridges us consciously to our Higher Self. In this place, we are connected to the angelic realm, the prophets and teachers and all light. We are not separate from all that is infinite, which is our God self. This state is accessed easily when we first wake up from a deep sleep, for we have been in these realms and our dreams consciously can guide us. In these states we are not attached to the ego. This state is where we create. This state of presence is where all of me lines up in the present moment and I co-create with God.

After the first episode with my heart, I immediately looked at what I was manifesting in my physical body and why this was happening. I know it all had to do with my own heart's love and my need to set boundaries for myself.

Being a medium for Spirit can take me away from my own needs and be a distraction from my own commitment to self. I would get caught up in that Spiritual energy and forget about this body. I was so wide open I would let anyone in – and that had to do with the non-physical world, too! Never could I have dreamt the test that would next unfold.

38

9-11 The Nation's Heart Attack

On the morning of September 11, 2001, I was in a very weakened and vulnerable state. The effects of the lightning strike had become so debilitating that my sister Colleen came down to Florida to help take care of me.

I was on the phone, talking about my challenges with my heart, when the caller said, "Turn on the T.V. and watch the Nation's Heart Attack!" Along with millions of others, Colleen, Steve and I watched as a plane flew into the World Trade Center. It did not seem real. It was like watching a big stunt from the latest action movie.

I wrote in my journal: " *I think sometimes we really can't feel the tragedies of this world unless it's in our own backyard. The most devastating disaster of my time just happened on live television. Yet life as I see it here on the little island of Anna Maria, looks as it always has. It is a quiet, peaceful place to live. It may look the same but I am sure that the tragedy that hit our nation is touching all of us.*

We can turn on the television and watch it all. We can touch the people that are victims of the nation's heart attack with one glance of our eyes, but can we fully feel the hurt, the pain, the suffering at such a darkened time?

Our nation's core – The Big Apple, New York City and Washington DC – has been attacked by the terrorists. These violent hate crimes, the dark forces, have brought America back to what is important. I see and hear the leaders talking of war against the terrorists, yet I see the hearts of humanity talk about peace and love and healing. I hear the religious leaders talk about our great God and the compassion of humanity's heart. It seems so big, just like the God I believe in. I hear about the heroes and the angels that walk in bodies on this earth, helping their brothers and sisters.

I listen to the president talk about war and yet I feel the pregnant pause of peace, where most of humanity has not jumped into attack, for they are feeling, listening and sharing. I see our nation's heart attack as the greatest gift to our world. We can be united as one and believe in all of humanity. I want to believe in bin Laden as one of God's children. I want to believe in the terrorists who have been brainwashed into knowing only hate and revenge. I want those in our nation to believe in their own selves and to touch their own rage and anger and see our brothers and sisters as abused and unloved."

I prayed a lot that day. We all did. In my sadness I held the space for humanity and tried to rest. That night, Spirit woke me up with the same voice, "Frannie..." This time there were many Spirits standing in my bedroom. So many, so many, so, so many. I was overwhelmed. I was feeling so vulnerable and physically weak. I could not participate. I said, "No." I had to say, "No." Again and again they called, "Frannie..." Again and again I said, "No."

Finally, morning came. Colleen came into the bedroom and said she couldn't sleep because she felt many spirits. Steve said he did, too. Colleen said she was frightened. I understood how she felt.

I felt them. And I felt my guilt. Part of me felt responsible – how could I not be an open channel for all these spirits that had just transitioned?

I knew that it was time for me to set limits for myself. Maybe this was a huge test from the universe. Could I take care of my own needs and let go of the outcome?

It was time for me to take care of my own needs in the physical body and love myself enough to let go and trust in the plan that was unfolding.

I sat with an open heart and an open mind and prayed for guidance. "If it is in my highest good to receive at this time, I pray for God to show me the way and in doing so, may I share the truth with humanity."

This is what came through:

"This is a time for all of humanity to remember the truth. How this truth is perceived is up to each person individually. There is only one reality. This reality is created from love or fear. The reality created by fear will always return you back to me. The reality created from love will sustain you as you live in a body.

Living in the body is the choice that is made to bring the truth of your soul into being. The soul knows that love is all there is. The ego mind believes you are separate from this reality that I am in you. I am this reality. I am the love that you are searching for.

Whatever is created in this world is created for you to choose your true state of being. You have the ability to be in love or in fear. You have the ability to stay connected to the truth of love or allow your own process to bring you out of the illusions created by your own belief in separation. You are not separate from Me and you are not separate from all that is created in this world. It is up to you to allow your own fears to be touched and embraced as you allow yourself to return back to the only truth that supports all that you are.

I am in the light, as I am in the dark. All is necessary for your soul's evolution. As you are in your heart, your mind will see the truth that the darkness will show you. It will bring you back to the original place of thinking as a spiritual being does hold the thought of the I Am presence. The moment is now. The moment of truth is here in the now.

What do you want in this very instance? You want peace and here it is. It is right here in your heart. It embraces the truth and the truth embodies peace. Let yourself remember why you came to be in a body. You came to experience all that you are. In experiencing the light and the dark part of yourself, you can understand why you experience separation. When you allow yourself to take responsibility for being here, you will return yourself back to your true nature.

You are like a child that has no past to create the present with. If you allow these times of darkness to be embraced by the past thoughts of pain and suffering, you will create more of the same. If you can be as you were as an innocent child, you can let go of what you think will happen and move along with the flow of nature. You will be a full participant in the evolution of this world. You can see this world as I do. It is a place where all can remember the truth of who they are and if you are made in the image of Me, then you are love. This love can endure the darkness and it can lead you to bring your brothers and sisters into the only true reality that is here to be created.

You are creating Heaven on Earth, but it will not be in the physical until you live in your heart. It is created in the heart of the one that knows that I am you. This ever-powerful love will not be destroyed and for all the ones that have left the physical world, their love and light is a part of you. Even that which you believe is evil or dark forces. These terrorists are the light and the energy of the love that you are all searching for. Be like the child and allow these so called tragedies to bring you to your own healing of pain and suffering. May it clean you and clear you of all that keeps you separate from the love that I am.

Hard times can bring you closer to me or further away. I assure you that you will return to the truth, for even if it takes this entire physical life to remember, your last breath will bring you to the truth that you are. You are the salvation and the remembering for many. Go and be all that you are and where there is judgment, let your true self remember that there is only one. Blessed be. I Am God and I Am the love that embraces all."

Let us trust in the process of humanity's evolution as we take care of our own dysfunctions and lost emotions. Let us clean up our own backyards and touch the children and our families and friends. Let us move through our own debris and clean our minds of hate and revenge so that we can feel safe to be in the world again and reach our heart's hand to touch our brothers and our sisters. Let us join hands with humanity as our hearts pray for peace and unity.

My favorite prayer book is *Illuminata* by Marianne Williamson. She writes:

"Our prayers for the world are our greatest contribution to its healing and rebirth.
Dear God,
Please send a miracle.

Into every country and every home, into every mind and every heart, may the power of Your spirit now trigger the light, activate our holiness, remind us of the truth within.

May a great love now encompass us, a deep peace give us solace... May the world be reborn.

Help us forgive and leave the past behind us, the future to be directed by you. Hallelujah, for You have the power. Praise and thanksgiving as You use it to save us, to heal us, to lift us from the past.

And we accept.

Thank you very much.

Amen"[23]

39

Live Simply

It would take another month after the enormous tragedy of September 11, 2001, for me to return to my work with Spirit. While I was still too weak to travel, I was confident enough in my physical body to provide a telephone consultation.

A few weeks after September 11, I was lying in bed in a meditative state awaiting a call from Shelley, who was going to call me at ten o'clock that morning. I like to get quiet and empty my mind before a session. She had called a few days before to ask for help. I was still feeling weak, but I knew that I am healed while I do my work with Spirit.

I wanted to be an open window for Spirit to move through and allow my gift to inspire her. In this quiet state, I began to feel Bernard, Shelley's husband in spirit, move into my consciousness. He sat comfortably beside me on the bed with his hands in his lap, leaning over to me. *"I want to talk to her. I want her to listen to what I want to say. I want her to hear me."* His energy seemed serious, he wanted to get his point across. I stayed in the peace and silence and then these words came:

"Live simply.

Bring your focus to the simple life.

That is where your happiness will be."

Bernard had died ten years before from a brain aneurysm. Their love for one another was a story in itself, and now years later Shelley was going through a dark time. She felt Bernard was trying to communicate with her but she could not hear him. She needed some guidance and wondered if she was holding him to this dimension with her attachment and love.

When she called, I felt a wonderful connection with her and looked forward to the session. Shelley was at a crossroads in her life and wanted to move forward, but felt stuck in her emotional body. After our session, I found out she and her husband had been the owners and designers of one of my favorite clothing stores in Toronto. During my career as a model, our paths had certainly crossed, but we did not know each other personally, a fact for which we were both grateful. Had we known each other, we might not have trusted enough to open up so freely in our session.

I answered the phone, knowing it was Shelley. I shared with her the information that had come through that morning. We were ready to begin, so I put the phone on speaker and sat comfortably, ready to receive without effort. These are the words that transpired from the session:

"Breathe... trusting in the communication of your heart in what you want to do in this portion of your life...

It is as if the physical body has so much to bring in, the Spirit wants to come in so fully but the physical body is not ready. It hasn't fully healed its fear. So aneurisms can be in the heart and they can be in the brain and other parts of the body that stop the flow of energy because the body in some way gives up and says that it is too hard to be a physical body.

And Bernard wants you to forgive him. He says you have forgiven in your mind but he wants you to feel it in your heart. It's not about forgiving him, it is about forgiving yourself for not living fully. In this instance that he is here with you at this time, you are to bring more of yourself into the world.

I am here as your gift of life. I am here to help many through you... My love is in you. I will help you to move into this stage of your life... I will communicate through you in your writing... in your communication beyond what you believe that comes through your mind. It is beyond it. It will come through your heart and you will begin to speak it. You will speak these words to help others. It will come in a book. It is most important for you to live in this body fully feeling this energy, this love.

It is easy for you to leave. I did choose to leave my body to help you and to help many. It is for you to realize that in this moment of forgiveness of your past you can fully embody the simplicity that our great brother St. Francis did teach us. It is in this moment in remembering that this energy of our beloved Jesus and in the light of the Christ be born again in every heart that you are a part of. Whether it is conscious or not, many in the future will be anchoring in this energy and in this moment. Be free to live in love, in peace and in harmony. This is what your life did bring you. This is what you choose not only for yourself, but especially for the children.

You are here to live in a body, to live this experience. It does not mean in this life that you will choose to live as a monk. It is for you to know that in your simplicity, in the simple moment of living in your heart you will choose to bring all these energies into your life. You will be free to live the truth of who you are. It is not that you do not know this in your mind. It is that you have not fully lived it in your body without me.

It is for you to know that seeing me as I was will never be; yet seeing me as I am will always be. I am always that energy within you. I am an energy within an energy. We are like twin bodies of energies. It is for you to know because you did experience that which we are together. You can experience it always within yourself. And for this next stage of your life in a body you will show others for they are here to remember this love.

Your life will not be what it was; it will be more of it. Let me go. You must fully let me go so that you can live fully as you are. And I am in you. I will be in you, living a vibration of truth that is yours. This is a contract that we did know before we came in bodies. This contract is going to change now, for the contract is known to you as divine. And it will change in this way...

You are here to be open each day to receive the information of the councils of light. The love that we have together will bring you to that. It is for you to know that you are now ready to live in partnership with another. It is for you to know that there will be children coming to you; they may not come through your body. It is for you to be open to be the living example of this love for children. It is in the written word that you will understand what this means.

I am honoring you, as I live beyond this world for it is you who has chosen to stay. Yet this choice was made a long time ago, my love. When I speak to you as my love, it is the union of the love of God. There are many in pain and suffering at this time. It is your compassionate heart that will bring the many energies of Spirit into this world through this physical presence.

It is first and foremost for you to feel it for yourself and then go to my family. Trust in that. For it will heal them. And hold my mother so that she can feel me. As the years that have gone by in the human world as you live, there is no time here. As we are in Spirit, being fully with you, we are with you more than your thoughts could ever know. We are with you deeply on every level with every body that you have. You have more than this physical body. You have many bodies on different levels. Your emotional body, your physical body, your Spirit, that are living in oneness and I am communicating with you in this place. I can walk into your living room and sit with you in conversation. Yet I choose to work on many levels to support you in your growth for as I am learning and remembering what our soul came here for, you will receive this information in your dream state. This portion of your life is to be lived present. To feel everything... I am in gratitude of your openness, to receive me beyond a body for in this place I am always guiding you and loving you. Know that the pain in the physical body pushed me closer to my Spirit and my divinity.

Blessings to you always, we are always together and you will meet many that are waiting to meet this love that you are. Understand that through the simple moments you feel more of God. I leave you with this truth. Feel me whole in you. I hold the part of you that longs for our physical connection. Trust that the way that I hold you now is God touching you and every part of you is loved and not judged.

Peace be with you my love."

Whenever I choose to assist Spirit in bringing messages to loved ones here on earth, I find that I receive at least as much as I give. It reaffirmed for me that guidance from Spirit can change your life, if you choose to listen.

Shelly chose to listen. The message she received from Bernard allowed her to re-open her heart and re-connect with the world. The love and energy transformed her. The love she shares with Bernard no longer serves as an anchor to her past. Instead it is a beacon that keeps her present and participating in her own life.

40

Happy Trails Harry!

Each year for the past three years, my soul sister Kristine and her husband Jacques have given me a trip to Hawaii. It is our retreat together and this year more then ever I saw that it was divinely set up for me. I know there is a plan and showing up for it always brings me more than I ever anticipate. I don't have a lot of material abundance of my own, or money in the bank, but I always seem to manifest these incredible opportunities for my soul's evolution and the experience of an abundant life. In so many ways I feel I am the richest person in the world and I am so grateful for my life.

Swimming with dolphins is what I love to do in Kealakekua Bay outside the house we live in on Kona, the Big Island of Hawaii. This is where the Humpback whales and dolphins come to birth their babies or to rest, because it has a sandy bottom. This year we swam with hundreds of dolphins at a time and the freedom and joy they showed me was life changing.

One morning we kayaked out to the middle of the Bay and there were whales swimming and breaching right there with us. Wow!!! My heart expanded - the thrill was so exhilarating. To be in the water with the whales so close was a new experience. When I looked down through my goggles to the bottom, I clearly could see sixty to a hundred Spinner dolphins at a time. They were fifty feet below me and the water was as clear as a swimming pool. In small groups they would come up for a breath and I would be a part of the pod. Then, they would leap, spinning out of the water and play with us. We would give them a leaf and they would flip it with their fins and bring it back.

I love watching their cute faces - they look like they have a constant smile. Their message is one of joy and peace. We honored these mammals by not chasing them or bothering them unless they came to join and connect with us.

One morning in the Bay I met my friends Michael and Karina along with Joanne, a woman who was born and raised near my home town in Ontario. It was a wonderful connection. Karina, who is a gifted flute player and healer from Germany, asked if she could do an energy healing with me using essential oils to clear out my aura and to bring more energy to my heart. While I believed that my heart valve problem was healed on many levels, I continued to hold the space for the physical heart to manifest the healing. So of course I accepted. During the session I experienced a vision of a man in my energy field. My mind wanted to try to figure out who it was; instead I just let my heart receive the beautiful healing energy. The love was expanding me and our exchange was sweet.

That night, my husband Steve called to tell me his dear friend Harry, who was only fifty-five years old, had just died. Steve had spent time with him only a few days before. Harry had told him he had some kind of heart problem and was experiencing so much pain that he was taking morphine. Steve thought Harry's problem might be like mine and wanted to share some of my detoxifying strategies to reduce his need for drugs. Now he was calling to tell me Harry was found dead watching cartoons on the television, with one hand in the cookie jar and a big smile on his face.

Steve was devastated and in shock. Later that night, as Kristine and I meditated and prayed for Harry, his family and friends, we felt his presence with us. I saw him in my mind's eye and he kept saying, "Everyone is so sad, everyone is so sad." In that moment I realized it was Harry's face that had popped into my energy field during my healing session earlier, but because I do not know him well, I did not connect, or I was not ready to connect.

Harry's son Timmy was living in Hawaii and was going to return to his father's home for the funeral. Steve talked to Timmy and they made a plan to bring Harry's ashes out to sea using Steve's boat.

I prayed and told Harry he could come to me if he wanted, to bring a message to his loved ones. Days later, I was back in Florida and babysitting my God-babies, Sarah and Daniel. They went down for a nap so I decided to take one too. I was in a deep sleep when Daniel woke up screaming. I bolted out of my unconscious state and easily settled him back down. As I lay back down, I felt the inspiration to write. I prayed and asked God to use me if I could be of service to help those who loved Harry.

Allowing the words to come through is easy for me, especially when my mind is empty and my heart is open. It really is like writing with your heart because the words just flow through without any thinking involved. That day was no different. I began to write and in the words and in my energy field, I felt Harry.

How did I know, you might ask? The answer is, I just know. That is how it is with Spirit communication. There is an inner knowingness that I just trust and when I let go of the ego that wants to stop me, I usually bring forth words or visions that touch me deeply and can touch others.

It's all about letting go and trusting in the next moment. If we could just live this way in all aspects of our lives, it would be so flowing, wouldn't it? The words are always of love and truth, and through me as a channel, I can learn or remember why I am here in a body. The gifts are numerous and I am grateful for the opportunities to share if another is open to reading or hearing the words or stories.

I did not know Harry intimately; yet, from the few times I had met him, I did know he was a 'Big Heart' and a gentle, sweet man.

We can all let go of who Harry was as a human being and know that he is now God's love moving into our lives. Harry is the love and light of God and we are the same as we carry on in our life and create more of who we are in this world.

These are the words I wrote as Harry inspires us to remember the love and truth in our daily lives.

(These words were written through me; yet I believe that Harry wanted these thoughts to be shared with all who knew and loved him.)

March 19,2002

Can you know that this state of being is for all to experience? Let the light in as I am with you here in the peace of your open heart. There is always love here and this is what all are looking for within their own lives. Let yourself let go of the thoughts of guilt for there is no such thing here. It is in the mind of the ones that believe that they are responsible for the hurt and pain of another. There is no one to blame especially in life because in death the truth revealed is that there are no wrong choices. There is no one to look upon with saddened eyes, for the eyes of the heart are always in love. Seeing that the moment is the perfect reflection leading all to their salvation, I now know the salvation of my soul. It is that I never had to be saved, for the God of my understanding is always with me. The God of love and peace would never turn itself away from me. So I do not turn away from you, even now that I have left the physical world as a body.

I am the living body of Spirit that will, for all eternity, be a part of your life. Let me join in with your heart and celebrate the life that is always birthing in each moment. The children birthed from me will be always embodying the energy that I am. Creating is going to bring more of me here through you. Whatever you do, bring this love that I am into your heart and share it with all who come into your life. They will feel the joy and laughter that has continued to inspire and bring passion to me. Even in the times of darkness, I understood that there was a reason for this life.

Your life is precious and it does not matter the life span in a body. What does matter is that you live the love that moves through you. Grace will embrace you and touch this moment that you realize that I will never be separate from you. Today is the day to celebrate all that has brought you together. My son will show you the way to the biggest truth that shines for all to recognize. My death has brought him to know the gift of love that never dies. Remember that the Spirit of me is part of you until we all are joined in the one ocean of eternal life. Find the joy in the simple moments of life and do not forget the ones who are in the present life with you, for it is in the joining of your hearts that the physical life becomes heaven on earth. Let the challenges of life show you that your choice to be here is to share yourself and your love in whatever way you choose.

Take care of yourselves and each other, for these lives you live are precious. You take nothing with you when you leave your body except the love that lives on and on.

Happy Trails for all.

Harry

41

Life Is Worth Living

We have been given a life and then we are free to make choices for ourselves. There are no wrong choices. Each choice brings an experience that we grow from and evolve from. For the past fifteen years I have focused on healing myself from the inside to discover who I am and what I want. I am now approaching the age of fifty – half the age my grandmother was when she died. Her body was strong and healthy. Her mind was alert and she was present right to the end. She used to hug me and when she did, her strength wrapped me with love. I wanted her strong, healthy body.

My grandmother was always an inspiration for me and our closeness touched me deeply. We enjoyed talking about the same things. She was fascinated with the Spirit world and psychic phenomena. I was free to share with her my abilities and my many experiences with the non-physical world. We were even able to meditate together and sometimes I would bring messages to her.

One day we talked about her death. She was in her early nineties at the time and we decided to have a sign or symbol she could embody when visiting here from the Spirit world. She said she would come as a blue bird. Grandma's favorite color was blue, so this was no surprise to me. I have always believed that birds were angels, anyway, because of their wings.

When Grandma died in her one-hundredth year, I was in Florida and unable to go back to Ontario for the funeral. Instead, I sat in meditation and prayer all that day, celebrating her life. After the funeral, family and friends gathered at my Aunt Therese and Uncle John's home where Grandma had lived a few years before moving to a nursing home. Those present began to share stories and my Dad told everyone about the pact his mother had with me, about coming as a blue bird to let us know she was with us in Spirit.

The whole time my dad was sharing the story, a blue jay stayed on the windowsill. This blue jay began moving all the other birds away as if to say, "This is my party and no other birds were invited!" She wanted all the attention.

All day long, the family members would joke and say they were going outside to be with Grandma. The bird stayed for the entire day on the windowsill and I know that day there was some magic in the experience. I was excited she had come. Many times since her death a blue jay has come when I feel my Grandma's presence or I just call for her from my heart.

Through my challenging days and nights with the physical health issues I experienced, I cried for help and prayed for Grandma, my guides, angels, Jesus or all of the above to come and help me in my despair. One night after feeling all of these emotions, I had reached the end of my tolerance with the physical symptoms. When I finally fell asleep, I dreamed of Grandma. I could hear her voice so clearly and there was so much light vibrating with every word she spoke. I awoke the next morning and told Steve that Grandma had come to me and shared some beautiful words of inspiration, but all I could remember was that it was about the body.

Later that morning, Colleen called and as I shared my dream with her I could feel Grandma's presence with me. Colleen felt it as well and I sensed that soon the words I had heard in my dream were going to come to me. At the same time, Colleen told me a bird was banging into her window. Birds have always been symbols of a message from Spirit.

Soon, the words began to come so I asked Colleen to write them down. As she moved into her office in the next room, the bird followed her and again started banging on that window. As I spoke the words, Colleen wrote them down. She was crying as we both experienced so much love in the communication. The bird left after these words came through:

"Sweetie (I could hear her voice in my head), continue to remember that whatever you choose to do, you may choose from that part of you that believes that this life is worthless or that this life is worth living.

I lived for my body so that my body would live – that my body would keep living for the dream. I did not touch it fully, as you touch it, as I am now as energy. You touch it in a body. Most people long for it and that is why they die. My will kept my body alive, to feel what you have.

Your body is alive because of your will. Your body was not strong. Your body stayed alive because of your will. You have touched Spirit and your belief in what is beyond this body. Surrender. Let this energy bring you to where you are to be.

It does not mean you have to die; yet every body has a life span that lives in time and space. You cannot fight. You can only be. Surrender in this great place and be. This force and power is who you are. It is who I am. It has no attachments.

Humanity believes that living in the body is utmost reality. It doesn't matter the outcome of the outer reality. It is the inner truth of a power that lives on and on beyond time. Allow your will to make the choices for the body as you allow the magnificence of your Spirit to be fulfilled. If for only a moment it is the greatest gift. This power is freed in the body when you touch all the parts that have lived attached to form – your identity, your beliefs.

Let this force of being heal all that is, for in this moment all is revealed and all is remembered. It is most difficult and most challenging for humankind to bridge the worlds we live in. Each step you have taken has brought the union of body, mind and Spirit. As you have witnessed the past, it is let go of as you let go of the feelings. Trusting in every step for 'Thy will be done.'"

As these words came through to me, I saw visions. One vision was of my Grandma at the nursing home not long before she died. She had watched a movie of the Holocaust and for the first time in her life had taken the event to a personal place. Up until then, she had always viewed the Holocaust in a detached way, without feeling any emotions. But now the wall had come down and her heart opened to the true feeling of this enormous tragedy. Afterwards, she went up to perfect strangers and asked for forgiveness because she was German. With her heart open, she wanted to share the compassion she now felt with everyone.

Then I saw a vision of Jesus on the cross and the words "Father, why have you forsaken me?" and then Jesus said, "Forgive them for they know not what they do."

As I know that the message was appropriate for me at this time in my life, I believe these words can touch a world personally as I share them. This life is worth living. The creation of these words has guided me closer to my truth in many ways. Grandma had a strong and healthy body, and that's what I would like for the next fifty years or more of this life.

42

Love Is All That I Am

I hear my father's voice on the other end of the telephone. "You can do it again, Frannie. You can heal your body yourself – just like you did before." I hear his love and his support and in this vulnerable sick place, I can be inspired by his love.

My parents have always believed in their children and allowed us the freedom to explore who we are. In this, I think they gave us the greatest gift. They did not force their views on us; they just loved us unconditionally. When I first became sick with chemical sensitivities, my dad and mom helped me research. My dad would go to the library and bring back every book he could get his hands on about nutrition and health. My mom created a safe place for me to be in my darkness, where I could also bring my children and know they were taken care of. I could go deeper into what I needed to do to get well.

Here I am again. I am here to go deeper into my self and find out where I am not plugged into my personal power, the universal life force that is my Spirit. I have another opportunity to experience a beautiful life.

"Dear God," I prayed, "show me the way and allow the truth to set me free." I received:

"I am within you. I am the heart that loves without conditions. I am the one that knows all of you. I am all that you are. Let yourself be free to know that in this physical world there are physical laws. The laws are for you and they guide you to your own salvation. These laws are universal and they are known within your heart, and your soul is the connection to these eternal truths. The soul continues to live on as energy as every part of you takes on the vibration of the unlimited energy that is your source. This energy grows as you allow your self to be known, as you allow your self to be uncovered by the mystery that empowers your state of being.

When you allow your true state of being to live in the present moment, all of the eternal truths are available for you to tap into. These truths are the mysteries that human beings have searched for. They are found inside your own heart and when you come upon them, it is you that will allow the truth to be told to you, for you. It is your own perception that will embrace these vibrations and the guidance is for you. How you interpret them is up to you. It is your life and as you share it with others, you bring the vibration of these eternal truths into creation. The creation is up to you.

How much of this energy can you allow into your physical human self? How many ways can you bring this vibration into this world you live in as a body? It does not matter in what form it is shaped into. It is a part of you that never is separate from you. The mystery is the presence of more of who you are as Spirit and the human form is the vessel for its entry into this dimension called Earth.

There are so many ways to say the same thing. That is where human beings get confused and distracted. Yet it is in feeling the experience of this energy that I Am and you will allow its truth to be known to you and for whom ever you share it with. It is for all of my precious children to return back to the path of the heart. To allow the heart to open even greater, in every aspect of your life. To know that this journey you are on is to remember the truth of who you are.

You embody the vibration of the creative force that is never ending when you are love and when you are loving. It is so simple and yet it is so complex. Return back to your heart and know that I am here for you. Whatever you ask for, you will receive. Know that it is you that must let go of it for it to be received. You are the image and likeness of me and that has no form, it only has the energy of love that is eternal. This physical world is blessed by this knowledge that is the bliss you are searching for."

Trust is what we are all learning – to trust every moment and let go into the next. There are no wrong choices. Sometimes that is tough to swallow because we want to blame ourselves or another for the choices we make. Sometimes there is pain, yet there is great pleasure, too. The words from Sri Nisargadatta Maharaj in the book, *I Am That,* explain:

"Do not pursue pleasure – or shun pain. Accept both as they come, let them go as they must... you will find in pain a joy which pleasure cannot yield, for the simple reason that acceptance of pain takes you much deeper than pleasure does. The personal self by its very nature is constantly pursuing pleasure and avoiding pain. The ending of this pattern is the ending of self. The ending of the self with its desires and fears enables you to return to your real nature, the source of all happiness and peace... When pain is accepted for what it is, a lesson and a warning, and deeply looked into and heeded, the separation between pain and pleasure breaks down, both become experience - painful when resisted, joyful when accepted."[24]

I know I am healing. Whatever that looks like, maybe I just have to let go even more into the mystery of the unknown.

I had a dream. In the dream I was with my cousin, Mark, but as I write these words I realize it represented my friend and medical doctor, Marc. Both are dear to my heart. In the dream I was walking arm-in-arm with Mark/Marc and he said, "You are going to die, but remember that your children are taken care of."

Now my ego could analyze the dream from fear and be afraid that I was hearing inner guidance; that I was going to die from this physical body. This could very well be true, but what I know is that I have peace. I feel that a part of me did die, the part of me that tries to heal me. I am taken care of. All of me is taken care of by God, even if I choose to trust in a doctor's care.

So I rest in God's love. I rest in my own love of Self. I am so grateful for all the love that is here in this world to tap into.

My life is the greatest gift of love as God shares it with me every step of the way. I remember someone once said to me, or maybe it was a quote I read, but it went something like this: *"When you leave this world you won't measure your life by the material successes – A man's life is measured by the love she/he has shared."*

I love myself today and I can share these truths that touch my heart with the world by living life fully. My journey back to self is ongoing and the pilgrimage itself is the sacred place. Each step I have taken on my path is important in itself for it is my life. I hold the picture of myself that God has for me in her image and likeness.

And in the next breath, I let go of my picture and feel that love is all that I am.

How Can I Attain This Feeling of Love
In All Aspects of My Life?
(A message from Spirit)

"*Can you imagine a world without fear? If you can, then you know it is your thought of fear that brings it into creation. It does not matter what is created in your life, if you can be so present with it and allow yourself to be open, you will not be in fear. You will not be in judgment of the experience at hand. You would be the witness of a life that brings you more opportunities to love and to be loved. It is during these very challenging times, you realize you are here to reach deeper into your own heart and ask for the truth. Your own truth is where you start. It does not have to be anyone else's truth and you can't expect the world to follow you. All you can do is accept your truth without judgment and then you will be more open to what this world is all about.*

You are here to live this truth and to allow yourself to be heard and felt. It is to be fully present with yourself and to be fully present with others. In the moment of full presence, you are the focus that brings all into harmony. Will the world follow you? Probably not, but they will never forget your light and your love. It is so freeing for you to live for yourself and in turn you are living life fully for the world. I am with you in all ways. Sometimes you cannot feel the love because you have left yourself. The part of you that still continues to seek safety outside is remembering who she is. You are the light and you are the way. There is only one place to be and that is in your heart. Allow yourself to heal for all that has forgotten the power of love."

My connection to Spirit will allow all of me to step into my life, into this body. This energy is what I can plug into at any time. It's not that I haven't done it, I think of it as another chance to do it all again. Instead of dying from this body, let the past completely die and plug into all that is now. With the birth of self there is a death, both existing as a whole.

Forgiveness can bring us to the birth of self - the true self that wants to live here on earth. We are here to reprogram and retrain our thinking from years and years of unconscious conditioning. You know there is a saying, "The past is history, the future is a mystery, that's why they call the present a gift."

This is where we are to be. To be here right now, we do not have to bring the past or future into this moment. This moment can change your life if you allow the experience to be just what it is - another moment in time. Life happens and the energy that exists around us is so powerful.

We are all evolving and growing. I watch television, talk to people and I see the consciousness in our world. It's all changing because we are changing. WE ARE THE CHANGE. The people I walk with in life are my heroes. I listen to their stories and I am in awe of the courage they have to get through another day. These women and men and children inspire me each day. Together we are all moving towards something greater... and that is ourselves.

43

Birth Or Death Brings Us Back To Self

"But whether small or great and no matter what the stage or grade of life, the call brings up the curtain, always, on a miracle - a rite, or moment, of Spiritual passage, which, when complete, amounts to a dying and a birth. The familiar life horizon has been outgrown; the old concepts, ideas and emotional patterns no longer fit; the time for the passing of a threshold is at hand." –Joseph Campbell

My brother is an independent filmmaker and a Professor of Film Making at York University in Toronto, Ontario. His style is unique. It is a personal interpretation of his life experiences through which he also brings in his Spiritual beliefs.

I received the video of his film finished in 2001 called *What These Ashes Wanted*. At the beginning of his work, Phillip explains, "The film resides in an acutely intimate time, a daily practice of loss that is not a story of surviving death but rather, of living death through a heightening of everyday experience."

I watched it for the first time knowing it represented his grieving process around the death of his life partner of fifteen years, Marion, who I have written about in earlier chapters. Her life and death continue to inspire me. As I watched the film, I witnessed the personal inner findings that Marion wrote of before her death and related them to my own search for answers about my inner journey and healing of my physical body. I also saw where I am different and how far my personal journey has taken me. I grieved some more as I felt again how much I missed her physical presence.

That night I fell into bed exhausted, only to wake up early – too early – in the morning with physical discomfort. So I just lay in bed listening to my inner voice. I began seeing a great many revelations for myself and a part of me was being pulled to the computer to write it all down. Truly I just wanted to roll over and go back to sleep, but that persistent inner voice kept nudging me to the computer.

Usually I will pick up a pen and write at these times. However, for some reason I felt I needed to go right to the computer. So I walked into the office in the darkness of early morning, and I switched it on. To my dismay, the screen remained black except for a little flashing light in the corner and the words, "computer board failure."

I sat there with my mind chattering, "The computer has crashed! I knew I should have backed up all I had written yesterday on a disk!"

After feeling the frustration and upset of maybe losing the finished manuscript that was filed in the computer, I began to think beyond that. Perhaps this experience might somehow be perfect for me right now. Perhaps it was a divine intervention, a kind of waking dream for me to see something more profound in its happening. I went to sit on the couch and just be for a moment. Not letting my fear take over, I just sat feeling everything.

After I first learned how to use this computer, I began to see how much it functions like our bodies and our lives. It has been programmed and runs as if it totally knows everything. The computer works without us consciously knowing what is going on or how it is all interconnected, just like our bodies, which automatically breathe, digest food, make new cells and so on. Of course someone has programmed all of the information and wired this incredible machine – almost as well as God made these amazing bodies we inhabit!

The more you use the computer, the more it gets filled with information, programs and all kinds of files. Much like our lives... the more we live our lives, the more we are filled with information and programs and data to run them.

Yet the computer is vulnerable. It can get viruses that will shut it down and there are times when it freezes, gets jammed up and just stops working. Fortunately, we can reboot the computer and usually it will work again as if nothing had ever happened. If it keeps crashing, we can simply replace the old program with a newer version to correct the problem. I realized that's how it is with me. I have been reprogramming myself to let go of old beliefs and patterns that are no longer needed and do not serve me, or shut me down.

I wondered, "where does the information go when a computer completely crashes?" (Hopefully you have everything backed up!) Likewise, where does all our information go when we crash, or become ill? I then started to think about the words that Marion had written before her death. Because my brother lived with her and was the kind of guy he was, he realized he was witnessing something greater than what it appeared to be.

Marion had many thoughts and feelings she had wanted to share about her process of living and dying. Phillip somehow managed to capture and preserve them in this film. Marion's words touched me so personally as I listened to the insights she had received in the process of being present with her death. Her conscious presence with her physical symptoms seemed to bring her to understand the mystery of her life.

In watching Philip's film, I also got to know my brother in a more intimate way. I saw how he understood the experience, having been present and witnessed Marion's last days in a body. He wanted the world to experience it also. Her Spirit lives on in his film and in our lives, just as our own Spirit will live on through the people we touch and the life we live. Life and death are so close and as we let go; "the time for the passing of a threshold is at hand."

Philip writes these words:

"I always thought we would grow old together. I found this photograph, which she took eight years ago... I do not know much about the actual place where the photo was taken, but that its taking coincided with a severe illness which we thought she had recovered from.

In a state of wellness, which has marked her last years, she traveled and purged the things she felt created her illness in the first place. Lodged somewhere in this darkened surround, lays her after image. If I could brighten up this part of the picture I might illuminate the condition of her death, the mystery of her life and the reason why at the instant of her passage, I felt peace with her leaving, a feeling I no longer hold."

It was Marion's peace that Philip felt. I know that peace for I have felt it when I have been with the dying. I know that peace within myself when I feel a part of me, an old way of being that does not fit in my world any longer, die. I feel connected to the vast immeasurable universal energy that is all around me and inside of me. I have touched it over and over again and it always reminds me of who I am. It reminds me there is something so much greater to be a part of and that I am beyond this body as Spirit.

There is a Cayce saying, "*You can not overcome darkness by struggling against it. You can only allow more light into your own life, thereby affording it less and less influence until darkness becomes absorbed into your light.*"

I sat in the dawn of the morning, feeling my fears of death once again. My husband got up and sat down beside me on the couch, asking me how I was. I shared my feelings and I shared the experience of the computer and my realizations. As he shared his own fears and his love, we joined in our hearts. Going back to bed, I laid in his arms as he slowly drifted off to sleep. Having his arms around me was comforting, knowing that our journeys are different but in this place of love we are the same. We came into this world with our own agendas and together we unfold our own mystery.

44

Christmas Carol

As I sit on the beach, I open myself to the beauty that is all around me. I allow my breath to bring me inside to ask the question, "What am I to do now in my life dear God?" As I continue to pray and let go of the busyness of the mind, I can feel myself expand beyond my body, yet my energy seems to be hovering just outside of me. I feel both and I am not leaving the physical world with my mind. I am present with all of my bodies. There are the feelings and emotions, there is the connection with the physical body and where I feel discomfort, there are the thoughts that pass through my mind and there is Soul – my true spiritual self that feels unattached to anything and free to experience peace and love.

In this place, I begin to experience a presence of love that expands my heart even more. There is a knowingness that it is Jesus and I see behind my eyes, with my inner eyes. I see with my feelings that are present within my heart. I see Jesus. He casually sits on the sand beside my feet and as usual, He is wearing his blue jeans under His robe. There is comfort with Him popping into my life like this. It is the most intimate relationship I have, because in that moment I am so fully with myself.

I begin having a conversation with Him on the inners. It is like mental telepathy. The information or communication is of energy and sometimes, in a few words, I hear so much. It is as if thoughts are placed into my consciousness or the energy has allowed me to tap into the information that is stored inside, just waiting for me to receive it. Jesus answers my question by saying; *"You are here to bring the message of love and light into this world. You are moving yourself into the world by being present. There is nothing you have to do but be here now."*

I have heard these words many times before. Yet this time I was hearing much more. In the next moment I could feel the presence of Debbie, Marion and my Grandmother (who are all in Spirit) as my mind expanded even further and my heart embraced the energy. I felt the energy of their Spirits as I expanded and felt even vaster and totally connected to everything inside and outside of me. I became the bridge between both worlds. In that feeling of total love I then felt my mind and in that instant I was pulled totally back into my body, aware of the tightness and pain in my chest. In the dense feeling of the physical body I could hear Jesus speak to me saying, "*When the mind of the ego begins to attach to the past you have had with these souls, then you are plugging back into the parts of your life you have not let go of. Then you get to feel it if you choose to.*" I asked Jesus why everyone could feel Him and He said it was because He was not attached to the past and He was guiding us all home to the truth that is within every moment.

In the next breath I felt myself letting go of the attachments to my Spirit loved ones and my whole being expanded even greater. It was my choice. When we attach to someone we are also tapping into their illusions or more of our own. When we experience without attachment, then we are tapping into the creative power that is always in us and we are being the vessel for Spirit. As I let go of my attachments, I understood this wisdom deep inside of me. In that moment I felt my oneness with Spirit. We can all listen to words that express the experience of non-attachment, yet for me, experiencing it that day, in that way, was far more profound.

I sat in this expanded presence and when I opened my eyes, I saw not only the beauty of life, I was part of it all. I felt I was fully grounded and fully present with every part of me and it was all okay. I was being the love and the light. I was experiencing myself being in the world but not attached to it. At this time I felt the desire to pick up my pen and write these words that were moving through me:

"*There is a purpose for all of you in this life you live. Recognizing the love in all things can bring you to peace. You are creating with God and in doing so, your responsibilities are in the choices you make. There are Universal laws that help you to create consciously. Yet when you are fully present within yourself, everything is being created out of love. It is your own ego agendas that keep you believing that this moment is not perfect. Let yourself be the vessel of the creative force. You will see the beauty when you feel how beautiful this moment is.*

You are not living in a world that is not conscious. You are living in a world where each person is making his or her own choices and when you take care of yourself, what is created will touch the world as it is meant to be. What you view as bad is only judgments on choices made. When you are awake and aware that you are responsible for every thought and every feeling, then every choice you make will be aligned with the will of God. The creation from that choice brings another experience to be all that you are. Accepting yourself and letting go can be the difficult challenge, for the ego mind will take hold of every thought you have had about yourself and the tapes of mistaken beliefs can spiral you into fear. The heart loves unconditionally when allowed to create in love in every moment. Know that whatever happens is perfect.

Many stay stuck in the moment by judgments that then create with the same energy. Being fully present with all of yourself inspires you to attract what you are. You are the image and likeness of God. Bless your creations for each one of them will bring you home to your heart where creation continues to be made manifest with love."

The moment I stopped writing and felt the beauty, a woman came up to me. She said she wanted to come over and talk to me because my energy was strong and she could see the light all around me. She introduced herself by saying she had been in an accident years ago that had resulted in brain damage. She told me her IQ was 82, which she explained was that of an idiot. She said that after her accident she had been working to heal herself. Since that time, she has been able to see energy and light and discovered that she could travel into people's dreams.

I felt as if I were talking with her without any thoughts moving through me from my past or future. Like I had no personality. I was just listening and witnessing the moment. She was so full of love and life and she sounded somewhat like a child. When I asked what her name was, she replied, "Christmas Carol." I said, "I am sure we will connect again." Then she left and went back to her chair and I went back to my writing.

I was still in that peaceful place, not even thinking of the experience. I was focused in my writing when I heard from way far away, "Bye! Bye! Bye!" I looked up and saw her yelling from across the beach with her arms flapping like a child trying to get my attention. She was with an elderly man with chubby red cheeks.

I believe God is using us all the time to be Her messenger. I had just experienced truth with Jesus and life gave me an example to live the truth received. Maybe Christmas Carol was an angel with an answer to what I had asked earlier on the beach. She was so innocent and happy just being with her so-called disability. Without holding herself back, she was like a child as she shared the love that flowed through her so effortlessly. She was an angel bringing me the answer to my question, "What am I to do now in my life dear God?" *"Just be here now!"* God said. *"Be like a child."*

It is in our child-like innocence that we find the keys to enter the kingdom of heaven. Happiness creates health in body, mind and Spirit.

45

I Am Not This Illness

As I walked into Dr. Peggy Manning's office, I felt something pulling me into fear. When I lay down on her table, Peggy, an acupuncturist and doctor of Oriental Medicine, began to test my body. She told me I had viruses in my heart and liver. I could feel the part of me that did not want to hear what she was saying. Inside I heard myself say, "NO! NO! I am not these illnesses anymore!"

At that moment I felt a light and energy hovering over me. I could see it in my mind's eye. As Peggy put an acupuncture needle in the top of my head where the pineal gland is, I felt an energy move through me.

This energy moved up and down my spine as I expanded into it. I felt myself let go of all thoughts of illness. While I was not in control of this experience, I could feel my breath moving fully and deeply into my heart. My chest and lungs felt like they were expanding. It's not that I was consciously taking in more breath; there was a power moving and flowing through me that was taking over. A vast river of love began entering into my heart that was so profound. The tears ran down my face. Peggy had been holding my hand and now that she was in the energy, she was crying, too.

After the experience subsided, Peggy asked, "How long did you feel you were in that state?" Without hesitation I answered "Five minutes." I was startled when she told me it had actually been forty-five minutes. When I got up from the table, I was still vibrating this energy in every cell of my being. There was no more heart pain. It was completely gone. I was filled with gratitude and felt more alive than ever before.

The experience continued for days and others around me felt the energy inside of them when they were with me. I felt this was a spontaneous healing. Something had changed inside of me when I said, "NO!" to my belief of illness. I took my power back as this energy moved through my heart; letting love in, even deeper. My physical health changed that day as I remembered to breathe into my heart.

There was a belief I needed to heal about being in this physical body. A part of my personality shifted into a greater awareness. Maybe it all lined up that day because I was finally ready to believe in the power of God. Now, months later, I continue to experience health in both mind and body. Do I have symptoms? Sure, sometimes. The difference is that I consciously choose to breathe fully into the presence and surrender to the energy that is always here. This absolute love of God is the power that heals all.

46

Who Am I?

My true identity is not the clothes I wear or the material things I have. This is a part of me that lives in this world. But if I lost these things I would still be me. I was born into this world with a body, a mind and emotions and the opportunity to experience myself as Soul and bring it fully into this form. We are here to be the best we can be. Our personalities and the choices we make can prepare us to start each day with a positive attitude. If we choose, we will see the beauty in ourselves and in the world around us.

My illnesses showed me where I was not fully alive in my body and mind. I am here to remember who I am in each moment of this life – living, breathing, thinking and creating from moment to moment. To choose to live authentically is to live in the truth of who I am.

It is in our everyday life experiences that our Spiritual strength grows. The sacred is in every moment, whether you are sitting quietly in meditation in an ashram or typing an email on the computer. There is a saying, *"Before enlightenment, chop wood and carry water and after enlightenment, chop wood and carry water."* The only difference in the experience of living is that you can have awareness... or not. We can see beyond the illusion of everyday living. Every moment up to this one is precious because it is a stepping-stone to the love and the opportunity to share it with the world. Sharing this love is seeing the truth of what is really going on.

Our life can become a moment-to-moment meditation. But we don't have to put ourselves in a quiet corner some place to see the sacred divinity of life. We can now choose to be awake in daily living and we can see, hear and feel God in that moment. We are guided in this place. This place can teach you about your ego fears and divinelove.

Life can be a continuous communication with Spirit. It is as natural to me as breathing. When I feel the non-physical world, I am in wonder of the power that moves through me. As I continue to evolve, I realize that the more grounded I am, the more present and unblocked, the clearer I will be in receiving messages that help me to live in more peace and love. I used to choose to be in such a deep, altered state when I meditated, that when the experience was over it was like a dream I could barely grasp.

Now I choose to be in my body and in my life in present time. For when each of us knows our own uniqueness as a human being, we are better able to connect with the universal life force and tap into this creative force. When we are present, we are participating and co-creating with God.

My illnesses, my relationships, my challenges of life all served to bring me to this present moment. Can I now stay present in the moment without leaving it to go to the ego mind, which can connect to the past? Can I breathe into the fullness that is always here to feel? My journey has served me by teaching me to listen to my own body, to hear my own call for love, the love we are all wanting.

This love that we are is only a breath away. Each day we can hear the call for love in humanity. I can hear it because I hear my own calling. Does it mean that I live like Jesus, Buddha, Gandhi, or the Saints? No, but I am living and praying that in my own love I can be the vessel for universal love and light.

I feel that the fountain of youth is our own ability to tap into this infinite energy and to understand and fulfill our own purpose in life. Our Spirit guides, our visions and our dreams can help us to understand what lies beyond the physical. We can choose to live in the present moment with an open heart and silent mind and be the remembrance of the true Self, the Self that is God's Love.

These are the times when we can tap into the truth of why we are here and share the energy of love in our own ways. In these challenging times when fear is standing along side of love, we are here to witness the transformation in ourselves and in the world and live the love in our own lives. We are the change and it takes us into a world where we can inspire and create with love. Jesus shared the Truth with parables, which are defined as: 'short fictitious stories that illustrate a moral attitude or a religious principal.' Through His stories, Jesus shared the truths of love to all who were open to them.

By design, our lives are filled with these experiences; our own short stories that shed truth can guide us to understanding and making choices. Changing the way we see things and learning to think and speak in a more positive way, can help us to review our life. It is the truth in the message that enables us to dissolve the darkness, to live in love, not fear.

Our stories are real, but can we see the truths being revealed? We can, if we choose to be the observer, to experience our stories in the same way that we watch a movie or read a book. From this place, we can witness our life without attachment to it. Like a reviewer, we can define and examine the plot, the themes and the symbolism so we can uncover the truth that is hidden within.

The stories on these pages and the messages I have received from Spirit are my own experiences. The lessons and guidance I received from them have changed my life. It is my hope they will inspire you to unfold your own mythology and see that life can be a beautiful thing!

Book 2

The
Simple Truths
Of Love

Sacred Poetry

Artwork by
Frannie Hoffman

Book 2: The Simple Truths Of Love
INTRODUCTION

My journey to find physical, emotional and spiritual healing has brought me the gift of trusting the empty space and silence within my own mind and heart. This is where I hear Spirit. This is where I feel Spirit. This is where I feel connected to my God self, my guide to the truth. In this place, I trust completely in the love as thoughts, words and visions flow freely through me. I have learned to trust this place and simply allow the power to move through me.

I believe we all have the ability to bring this energy of God through in our own special way, whether we are a dancer, a painter, a sculptor, a chef, a renovator, or a child playing dress-up. No matter what our way is to bring through this creative energy, it is our connection to it that brings healing to ourselves and others. This connection is through our heart. I have learned there is an even greater power when two or more are gathered and I have come to believe in the gift of group energy.

Over the past thirteen or so years, I have facilitated many circles of women and men on their spiritual quest. As we go inside as individuals, we are each able to feel the support of the group that creates a safe place to touch ourselves inside in an even deeper way. Meditation, whether it is guided or in silence, brings an inner stillness where we can hear God speak. In this place within the emptiness, the experience is the love of the Beloved. As the Sufi poet Rumi says so beautifully, *"Beyond all ideas of right thinking and wrong thinking there is a field, I'll meet you there."*

This space within you and me is the same, but the way I express it is my gift to you, and the way you express it is your gift to me. All of the words and visions and thoughts that have come through me either while with a group or alone with myself, have inspired me to live in love and truth. I freely and joyously share the words of love that have brought me truth and taught me to live in a more conscious way. These words came from God. I believe they came through me so I can share the message with you. These words continue to help me live in love. The words are simple, yet the depth of meaning is up to each to interpret.

The non physical world has inspired me, and continues to inspire me every day of my life. I can feel a presence of Jesus, Mother Mary and the Angels, the masters, my guides, my loved ones in Spirit and all the light beings of the non-physical world. Come and meet me in this field of infinite possibility, where Spirit shares the simple truths of love.

Frannie

She Speaks From The Inside

You are perfect just as you are.
Receive the gift of the moment
for you are worthy of the love that is present.
There is so much to be a part of, and it is all within you.

Stop and feel the breath move you into the emptiness
that fills you with everything that you need.
Nourish yourself with the energy that exists
because you are here.

You are the giver and the receiver.
I am inside every part of you
and I am the remembrance of this true nature.
Discover that in every moment all you need is here –
to be the lover of all the love
is to be the presence of the presence.

There is a story that you are here to tell.
It is a story of a little girl
who begins to remember a part of herself, her true self.
This little girl then begins to share it with others
and then something stops her from sharing
and she stops to listen,
she stops to feel
and she stops to hear.

She hears silence. It is still.
She hears silence. It is soft.
She hears silence. It is delicious.

She waits for the voice to speak to her
and then one day in all her silence,
she becomes the voice.
She begins to speak from the inside.
When she speaks, she is hearing at the same time.
It is all coming from one place within her being.
It just doesn't seem that important to talk anymore.
Yet when she does, it is because she is hearing at the same time.

She begins to move out into the world again
to share herself from this inner place.
It is her heart that is speaking and hearing at the same time.

Silent voice of Spirit, I am,
I have come to share my truth with you.
There is only one of us here experiencing as all mankind.
Let us join in the silence and voice our oneness
as love penetrates every part of existence.

The little girl is now all grown up.
She is still being the silence that wants to speak.
As she listens, she shares the truth with all she meets.

Silence speaks the heart of God.
Open your mouth and let me touch this world,
for this world waits for you patiently
as you arrive on the silent wings of time.

Divine Love

The greatest gift is your presence.
To be here, like the rain,
that showed up here to touch us,
To touch the earth.

Bring your attention here.
This moment can be the moment
when creation is activated.
The same energy
that God created this world
and all humanity with.
The same energy
is in every moment.
Presence is an experience
felt deeply within
your own heart.
This is Divine Love.
This is God's gift to you
and it fills everything.

It takes courage to be vulnerable, to let go of control, to be so present with yourself. It does not matter what challenges are showing up in your life. You have free will to choose the path of light and awareness. You have the power to increase or decrease spiritual light in this world. You are the absolute equal of this divine love presence.

The world is a mystery. Your mind can try to figure everything out but in the moment of being present in your heart, your presence is creating. Every moment is creating and your vibration of energy is moving into this world and beyond it. It is the same energy that has created the sunset and the sunrise. It is so full. Soul chooses from this place to be full.

The next moment of life is the opportunity to share the wisdom of this presence of love. This is the dance of creation. This is the dance where humanity is in union with Spiritual light. The light helps you to see. Without this presence of Spiritual light, you might have trouble seeing the love that is standing right in front of you. The rain is but a dance upon the earth, no different than your presence. The moment before the rain is released to dance upon the earth, there are clouds, so dense, so full. It is wanting to be birthed, to be free, to release its energy.

Human experience is the same as nature. One drop of rain holds the energy of God. It is feeding you as it feeds the earth. You walk, you talk, you paint, you sing, you dance, and you share yourself with this energy. It is to be shared. Like the sun, it radiates its presence, dispersing its energy wherever it may be.

You are the expression of Divine Love awakened in this dimension when you choose to be the Presence. This presence is love, respect, kindness, beauty, truth, wisdom and much more.

Empty yourself and become vessels to receive Divine Presence. The more love you give, the more you will receive. Every moment is the opportunity to be Divine Love with your thoughts, words and actions.

**Because you are here,
someone is loved,
someone is loving
and someone is love.**

The Sound of God

The sound of God is heard in your true awareness. When you were in the womb you smelled God, you tasted God, it was in you and all the sounds outside of you came into this body with one belief to heal.

What was that belief? You have wrapped it in many garments, but the one belief was that you were separate. But you see beloved ones, the purpose of this lifetime was to be so aware of it, that you chose the truth because you began to experience full awareness. Each one here is holding the energy for the birth of the true self, and that is what you will be seeing in your world, in your life. You will be this energy as the womb of God birthing the true essence of humanity.

If you are distracted by the mind of the ego, you will not hear the sound of God in the silence of your being. Silence has sound and every sound you will recognize, in every word spoken, in every experience of this physical dimension. The sound is heard through your ears connected to your heart, and all your senses and pure awareness is attuned to the vibration of God. If you lose your sight, you will see. If you lose your smell, you will smell. If you lose your hearing, you will hear.

It's an inner energy that is a true sound. So many have lost their sight so they could bring into their inner being the true sense of seeing. Do you hear the sound of this one inner voice, or the sound of the birds, or the sound of the wind, or the sound of rage? You would hear the sound of God when you are the presence of all that is. You can feel it in this moment, you are anchoring it, and each of you is anchoring it in the physical body.

It is the remembrance, beloved ones, not the journey to it. It is remembering your journeys of being now, it is right now in this moment. Trust that your body knows how to be. It knows how to let go, it knows how to become One. When you are in love, you are being it. In every word, in every touch, in every scent and in every taste is the nectar of God. To be in love with this dimension is to merge your spirit with it. To be so passionate about living in this body, in this energy of love and then to share it with the world.

In this place there is no attachment to how it is, it is being it. Like an orchid, it is being it with its full passion. It has a scent, it has a color and it has a radiance. It has a physical presence of God. Unless you know this passion in you, it is not being shared. It is your experience that is touching God. It is your experience. God touches the world with you, becoming you in this pureness. It is bliss. It is a freedom to be the expression of all knowingness.

Find your own sound and let it move from your heart and create the sound of God that you are. The sound is what anchors this energy. As pure conscious beings, you are physical bodies anchoring the vibration of God presence into remembering.

Feel it, smell it, touch it and know it. And when one of your senses is not anchoring it, know that another of your senses will. Trust your body and trust who you are. You will never let yourself down or abandon yourself if you are in your heart.

Find your own sound and let it move from your heart and create the sound of God that you are.

Inner Space

The house is falling down but the I AM is still standing.

Our security does not lie in the physical world, it is within our being.

After the death of parts of Self, God holds me in that peace. When I know the peace for myself, then I can be that joy and peace for others.

To know this inner peace, is to share it. Come back to myself, come back from the chaos of life. Create from this place of peace and all will come and drink with me.

Open your hands as you open your heart. Breathing fully from your belly. As the breath enters you, allow yourself to touch all the places that are longing for love. Trusting and allowing, as the activity of the mind rests in your heart, because you are willing to be here.

Welcome your guides and angels and your spirit loved ones. Your heart knows their existence.

You are the carrier of the flame. We, together, choose to be like nature, forevr flowing eternally. This space is everything that is your future. It is every step you take, into the depths of the earth, that carry all the memories of your ancestors. You are here to know this peace, and this peace is the J Am.

There is no denying it as you touch it. You do not have to fall asleep again to awaken into this place. You have chosen to be awake. To be here. You have gathered the clothing that you need and the shoes that you will wear and the staff that keeps you touching the earth. You are not alone, ever, not alone.

The wind is your greatest companion. The birds will sing for you. The energy of the sun is always shining, wrapping its arms around you, even when you do not see it.

J Am the heart of humanity and when you are hungry there will be another that will feed you.

There is no separation in the giving of this love. You do not have to be perfect in your knowingness to receive gratefully the gift of humanity. Humanity holds the gift and truth of the divine, even when you believe they have forgotten.

The gift may be the darkness that you have forgotten to touch. The silence is the words that speak greatly the truth when you show up and you let everything move through you. What a blessed gift, because you are here and you believe in yourself.

It is your choice to close the door to this truth of self and the true reality. It is so vast within your being. How would you ever think of keeping yourself from it? But you do. Join humanity within the vastness of your heart and allow them to awaken when they see your magnificence.

This experience becomes your path.
Your feet know where to walk.
You are guided.
You reach outside of yourself to touch.
Your touch will warm the heart of humanity.

Silence

Silence wants to be
touched by you.
As you show up
for yourself,
your Self prays with God.
And prayer is your intention
to be fully present.

Life is being the gift of being present. If you are not being present you are dying to be reborn again.

It is never ending. It is fully being.

If you are not happy, sit with yourself for a moment and breathe into that place that truly knows who you are. You are here to be happiness. Whatever that means, it is your experience to live.

No one knows greater than you. Yet, you continue to walk around in circles, around yourself. It is your own self that you are meeting.

You do not need to hide in a sanctuary on the mountain top. You do not have to be in the temples surrounded by like-minded individuals to hear God speaking.

God is speaking with every word you speak. You continue to attract in your life what you believe is imperfection. If you could know your perfection and feel it within you in every breath, that is what you would see and experience in another. They would be your beloved again and again. You would fall in love with yourself.

It isn't falling in love with another. It is falling in love with yourself. All the parts of you, especially the parts that believe you are separate from the Divine.

These are the parts of self that hold the key to your own resurrection. Your salvation is within your own heart. Free humanity by freeing yourself. Fill your bodies with thoughts that are the vibration of the truth of who you are. Not the truth of society that believes in fear and separation and death.

And as your hands be open, your heart be open. You enter this world with your eyes open and there you see with your heart and you hear with your heart and you smell with your heart. Your senses are serving you to be God in a body.

And there are more senses to develop if you allow them to be. The silence of your mind creates telecommunication. Everything that you think is in your energy field.

It is only your own denials that do not hear the truth. Be ready for the truth and not be afraid of the false truth.

That is why you shut yourself off because you are afraid of the fearful thoughts of humanity. Yet if you know that they are not real, you will hear the truth that is in every moment guiding you. That is this energy that walks into a room before you enter. It is the energy of a sunset that comes to you before the sun sets and after it sets.

This is energy and it is who you are. And if you are not present with yourself you will miss your own ascendance.

It is right here. Trust in the guidance that speaks to you. Acknowledge the presence of your guides and masters and spirit loved ones. They are here loving you in gratitude that you are this present with yourself.

Because you are here, all the presence enters this moment. When you shift your paradigm into the center of your heart, wherever you go, God is entering.

Silence wants to be touched by you.

Flowing Into More Parts of Self

Life continues

It is the ebb and the flow

A letting go and a contraction

A beginning and an ending

A continuous circle of creation.

Life continues and it is the ebb and the flow, a letting go and a contraction, a beginning and an ending; yet it is a continuous circle and you are the one that decides when a creation is at its completion. And in the next moment you can realize that nothing really does complete. You decide to continue it or to move into another direction.

Everything you do is full in itself. It flows into another part of itself. That is what you are doing in every moment of your existence. You are flowing into more parts of yourself and it is a continuing process of evolution. If it were your time to die in this moment, would you think that your life was not completed? Would you believe that you were an unfinished piece of work?

You are eternal and you are full in your presence and in this moment you are a part of the whole creation of God. There are no limits to what you can create in this moment yet all that is created is full and complete within itself. As you allow yourself to be fully here in the moment and feel the presence within you, there is only a vast amount of infinite possibilities in which you can bring this presence into being.

Yet, it is enough just to be. It is enough to allow the moment to express who you are and to be in touch with the love that is for always. You can take everything that you do and bring your full presence to it and you would see that it is a perfect part of creation. You would know when to move into another direction or not. You would be aware that this moment is unfolding just as it is planned.

Be with your moments and trust that you are exactly where you are supposed to be and that it is perfect. Trust in your dreams for they become reality when you allow your conscious presence to be present with them. Some people are artists and their work of art is in the moment of creation yet it may not be recognized until the artist has died and the world is ready for the gift of that persons' creation. Does that mean that this person did not complete or finish what he or she came here to do? No, maybe the death of that person was the ending of the portion of creation in form and now the creation continues in Spirit.

It is for you to remember that it is your choice to bring that part of you into the world in whatever way you choose. It is your choice to move that part of your creation into the world whenever you choose.

It is all for you.
The timing is the birth of that part of yourself
that is ready to be birthed
into this world you live.
Flowing into more parts of yourself.

There's Only Love Here

There is only love here.
As you acknowledge this within your mind
then your heart embraces this truth.
When you feel this love in your heart
then your mind acknowledges this truth.

Can you imagine in this moment that you are this love?

You are now being this love and everything in your life is the experience of that which you are affirming within you in this moment. It is so simple and yet you leave this truth and allow the ego mind to be the power over the only reality that lives in fullness within you in every moment of your existence in this body.

Your breath can connect to this true reality and love is healing you now. Each and every one of us can affirm this vast presence of love that God has birthed within our hearts. Every moment can be the affirmation of this love as the mind remembers what the heart does know.

It is the mind that we are here to heal and when we heal the mind of its ego fears, we free the heart to live in fullness and complete wholeness. As we allow ourselves to remember this truth then we are the remembrance for all of humanity.

It is not up to us to change the world, yet in our own healing the world becomes the reflection of our inner being. We are not in reaction anymore to the outside world for we can be that space within our mind where our hearts embrace the world in unconditional love.

If ever you feel yourself disconnected from the love, know that you are on your way back to remembering. It is in being in the moment of truth that you are giving yourself the chance to return back to your heart. In your heart is God and in this place divine love is your true reality.

Praising the moment in love can bring more love to you and heal the mind of the negative beliefs that have kept you in separation from the true reality.

The truth is that this love of God is within you in all ways.

The Ego Disguises Itself as the Knower

The ego disguises itself as the knower.
Here is where I battle with my demons.
The heart embraces the wisdom.
The wisdom is in the space
where sacred mystery lives.
Letting go of everything that I think I know,
allowing the knowledge to be.

It is right here now.
In the silent mind
the truth is revealed.
Let me be still
so that I can hear it's telling.
Let me be here now,
in this moment, within my heart.
In the stillness the Spirit resurrects
and the love heals all.

True Partner

Just as a tree, standing in its fullness, knows it is God.
So it is with you, knowing who you are.
You have come to bring union.

You are the sacred.
And in this knowingness
let yourself be on the earth being heaven.

Let go of everything that you are attached to.
Everything that you think is your source.
This source is in you creating your life.

You are the sculptor
shaping form to be the vessel of light.
And every part of your life is that reflection.

You are the breath of God.
When you breathe consciously,
you feed yourself with truth.
And it touches every part of you that does not know.

The wisdom of the heart
is not wrapped up in the ego, it is wrapped up in the light.
It becomes the partner for humanity.
It becomes the partner with nature.
It becomes the partner with all creation.

Just as a tree, standing in its fullness, knows it is God.
So it is with you, knowing who you are.
You bring freedom into the world as you believe in yourself.
You have come to bring union.
Your expression as personality
is the vessel that brings God into action.

For energy moves through you as you are creation.
Viewing life from the inside, you become the witness –
remembering God has created this perfect world
and everything in it. It is all good.

I am your heart that looks into the eyes of humanity.
When you know it, you reflect it for all.
Your presence becomes the Light and the way.
For as I take your hand, beloved one,
and you reach out to walk with humanity,
my hand touches all
and my heart ignites the world
through your heart.

This is the greatest love affair.
You and God.
God and humanity.
God and nature.

You have come to bring union.

Heart

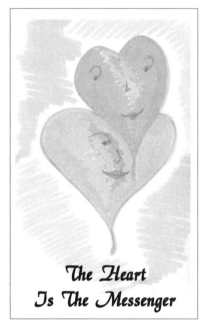

The Heart Is The Messenger

What is so predominant in the mind that takes precedent over the heart?

We still believe that we are to be punished and we still believe in shame and guilt. We still believe that we are bad girls and bad boys so we attract in our life people that reflect that for us. Instead we can say, "What an opportunity to bring peace to ourselves and ultimately to bring it to humanity." It all starts within our own individual heart.

Let heart be in every part of you. It is like waiting for God to show Her face. Can we be so patient with ourselves? Breath into the places that have forgotten that we are love. Your breath will take you there. And your consciousness will touch that place holding your fears, the darkness.

It is like waiting for the sun to set, knowing there will be colors to light up your being. And even if the clouds rest upon the sun, that energy is there, the beauty of God. And it takes great faith to know this. To wait for the opening. It is created in your open heart. The physical manifestation of clouds can move you inside to see the light of that sun. For its waves of energy illuminate your inner vision.

Maybe you do not see, but you feel this light as it dances within you. Touch it, believe it, and it becomes your power. Your presence gives you strength. You can walk upon the earth without attachment, yet you touch everything with your heart. For its treasure brings you to the compassionate heart.

This is where you hold humanity. This is where you heal humanity. This is where the mind is the servant to the heart. It is where the personality is the garment you wear over your soul.

It does not matter the clothes she wears. It does not matter the garment he has covered himself with. The labels, the names, it does not matter. It is what is inside that shines through when worn with an open heart.

If you truly want to know God, stand in this vulnerable place within your own heart and allow another to be the same. Even if you stood in front of a tree with that same willingness you would be with yourself as true as truth can be.

And that which you hide is a great teacher. The place you cover over and over. Be in your heart. Open to love yourself as God loves you. And what is birthed in this place, when you hold your fears with compassion, is peace.

Have faith in this energy that is your life. If it is plugged up with residue of the past, breathe into this place as you give life to yourself. Let that energy birth forth and move up your spine and move into the places that have held on to the belief that you are not worthy.

The heart is the messenger. It is the one that holds the information without judgment, without separation.

**It is the heart that holds the truth
that is whole in the moment.
You may believe that it is entering
through the mind of the knower
yet it enters through the heart
of the be-er.**

Express Me

Let Me move through your physical body.
I am the sound you hear, as I am the breath you breathe.
When you allow My presence to be,
you allow divine love into this world.
All wait for you to show up for I will be known through your heart.

It is your own forgiveness that heals your heart.
The living brings up the very thing that inspires you to be full.
The dying brings up the very thing that inspires you to be full.
Both are parts of the whole that create oneness.
Every breath will bring you into the present,
where all of life and death exists.
You are here to accept it all,
for it is the fullness of being here now.
Your own acceptance forgives.
You are the living expression of love.

Express Me.

Praise

Welcoming nature with open arms, you dance upon the earth.
And you travel like the wind, getting to know all the parts of you,
as you bow to nature and its magnificence, as it bows back to yours.

Everything you touch outside of you is you,
the color, the texture, the fragrance. Beautiful, divine, free, like a butterfly.
Your wings embracing the wind, as your heart is loving creation.

So Full Your Being. So Vast You Are.
Your heart speaks the silent truth of love.
Your presence is communicating God.
That is who you are, this energy. It moves into every part of you.
It now weaves into the earth giving it its beauty.

Perfect peace, unfolding the butterfly's wings.
The color that you are is being shown to the world
with your eyes open, with the smile of your heart,
with the touch of your hand.

The heart knows its true purpose of being is to be in love.
There is no greater truth. Praising the moment in love can bring
more love to you and heal the mind of the negative beliefs that have
kept you in separation from the true reality. The truth is
that this love of God is within you in all ways.

Your life is the opportunity to share truth.
How you interpret it, how you form it ... it is your choice.
It is your life that you form. The truth is the energy of divine love.
In love you praise God.

Be Not Afraid
For I Am With You

Be not afraid to be powerful.
Be not afraid to know what you desire
   to create in this world.
Be not afraid to allow your own self
   to live fully.
All parts of you have brought you
   to this moment.

This means the light, as well as the dark.
This means that everything and everyone outside of you
has brought you to this moment, to true enlightenment.

   What does enlightenment mean?
   It is the ability to stay in your heart no matter what the moment brings.
It is the moment of remembering that everything is possible. This experience
of love will bring you peace wherever you go and whatever the experience will
be.
   There is no fear of destruction, for in the heart you know that what is
real cannot be destroyed. It is of value to you as a human being to be aware
of all the parts of self that are within you and outside of you. This means that
all the people outside of you are a part of you, as you are a part of them. It is
for this reason that any attack on another human being would be an attack on
oneself. It is to say that even the loveless thoughts that are created from past
hurts and pains can be projected on the world if not owned and accepted by
your heart. It is the thought of guilt that seems to feed the part of you that is
in denial of your true self.

It is the true self that is here to live fully as you live in your heart. Living in one's heart is acceptance of all that is in the moment.

As you feel the guilt and shame of the past, can you love yourself so fully? Knowing that in the next breath you set yourself free as you give the pain to Me. Give to Me the belief you have of yourself that does not seem worthy of My abundant love. In doing this, you set yourself free. The one you keep in bondage by your feelings of lack and separation is also free.

This is the moment to rise up into the light and touch all that you remember in this love and let go. You will find your way back to the truth, for I believe in who you are.

You are a part of Me, part of the light that passes through time and space, where all is made clear to you as the mystery of the universe.

The mystery is felt as this vast place of nothingness where all knowledge is remembered. I am impersonal to all humanity. Yet I am formed through your person as your personality births the truth of love. Every heart is the open doorway to greater being and union with the divine light that is eternal.

This journey to self has brought you the SELF that embraces the pain and suffering of the world. Your heart remains to be the giver of light in the world that believes that abundance is the material world.

Know within yourself that you have lived in the truth of who you are and no one outside of you can betray this truth. You can allow someone else's fear to lead you back to separation or bring you into a compassionate heart.

As you listen to humanity with an open heart, this acceptance is unconditional love. Their truth may not be yours, yet the light is in all and each will be brought to their own salvation.

In one experience there can be a trillion different perceptions and this is all based on the individual life experience and lessons.

As you accept yourself, you are accepting another. Feel the freedom that you breathe as you allow the outcome to be made manifest for all.

Be not afraid for I am with you.

END NOTES

1 John R. Mabry, *The Little Book of the Tao Te Ching*, Element Publishing, p. 27

2 Harvey & Marilyn Diamond, *Fit for Life*

3 Phil Thomas, Beyond Theory. Edgar Cayce's Natural Health

4 Louise Hay, *Heal Your Body*, Hay House, Inc., p. 5.

5 Helen Schueman, *A Course In Miracles*, Foundation for Inner Peace, p. 77

6 Gary Zukav, *Seat of the Soul*, Fireside Books/Simon & Schuster, p 138

7 Dr. Michael Ryce, Audio Tape

8 Jim DeMaio, *Helping Not Fixing*, Life Transitions Inc., p. 23

9 Swami Sivananda Radah, *Kundalini: Yoga for the West*, Timeless Books

10 Caroline Myss, *Sacred Contracts*, Harmony Books, p. 26

11 Solara Antara Amaa-Ra, *11:11 Inside the Doorway*, Star-Borne Unlimited, pp. 18 & 24

12 Gary Zukav, *Seat of the Soul*, pp. 138 – 139

13 Oriah Mountain Dreamer, Poem "The Invitation"

14 Wayne Dyer, *10 Secrets for Success and Inner Peace*, Hay House, Inc., p. 28

15 Nelson Mandela, 1994 Inaugural Speech. Quoted from *A Return to Love*, Marianne Williamson, pp. 190-191.

16 Paul Ferrini, *I am the Door*, Heartway Press, p. 9

17 Ibid, pp. 12 – 13

18 Elizabeth Kubler-Ross, *Death And Dying*,

19 Wayne Muller, Sabbath: Finding Rest, Renewal, and Delight In Our Busy Lives, Bantam Books, p. 6

20 Wayne Dyer, 10 Secrets for Success and Inner Peace, p. 10

21 Dr. Jim Martin, New Advances in Natural Health & Healing

22 Helen Schueman, A Course In Miracles

23 Marianne Williamson, *Illuminata*, Random House, p.207

24 Sri Nisargadatta Maharaj, *I Am That*, Acorn Press,   p. 277

About the Author

Frannie Hoffman is a spiritual intuitive, writer, and artist, and an extraordinary facilitator. Through her meditation circles, writing, and compelling lectures and seminars, she motivates and empowers people all over the USA and Canada by her personal and honest expression of life and Divine Spirit. She has devoted her life to helping others tap into their own spiritual power, to take responsibility, to create and inspire personal empowerment, and to experience themselves as Divine beings.

Born a triplet, Frannie graduated from the University of Waterloo in Ontario Canada, with a Fine Arts Degree. At age seventeen she began her modeling career and soon became an international top fashion model based out of Toronto, Canada. She followed this career for fifteen years before the devastation of environmental illness forced her to give it up. With her very life at stake, Frannie chose to allow this shift to direct her attention inward, and so discovered the true purpose of her life, and her mission in this world.

She has raised two children, Luke and Lane, and now resides with her husband Steve on Anna Maria Island in Florida.

Frannie is available to facilitate meditation circles, retreats, and workshops, as well as private counseling sessions.

To contact Frannie:

Write to:
Road Signs Productions
P. O. Box 374
Anna Maria Florida 34216
USA

www.FrannieHoffman.com

E-mail: arayasunbooks@aol.com